# PSYCHOLOGICAL RESEARCH METHODS
## AND STATISTICS

Longman Essential Psychology
Series editor: Andrew M. Colman

# PSYCHOLOGICAL RESEARCH METHODS AND STATISTICS

EDITED BY

*Andrew M. Colman*

LONGMAN
London and New York

**Longman Group Limited**
Longman House, Burnt Mill
Harlow, Essex CM20 2JE, England
*and Associated Companies throughout the world.*

*Published in the United States of America*
*by Longman Publishing, New York*

© 1994 Routledge
This edition © 1995 Longman Group Limited
Compilation © 1995 Andrew Colman

This edition first published 1995

ISBN 0 582 27801 5 PPR

*British Library Cataloguing-in-Publication Data*
A catalogue record for this book is available from the British Library.

*Library of Congress Cataloging-in-Publication Data*
A catalogue record for this book is available from the Library of Congress.

Typeset by 25 in 10/12pt Times
Printed and bound by Bookcraft (Bath) Ltd

# CONTENTS

# NOTES ON EDITORS AND CONTRIBUTORS

ANDREW M. COLMAN is Reader in Psychology at the University of Leicester, having previously taught at Rhodes and Cape Town Universities in South Africa. He is the founder and former editor of the journal *Current Psychology* and Chief Examiner for the British Psychological Society's Qualifying Examination. His books include *Facts, Fallacies and Frauds in Psychology* (1987), *What is Psychology? The Inside Story* (2nd edn, 1988), and *Game Theory and its Applications in the Social and Biological Sciences* (2nd edn, 1995).

FRANCIS C. DANE is Associate Professor and Chair of Psychology at Mercer University in Macon, Georgia. He currently serves as secretary/treasurer of the Society for the Advancement of Social Psychology; his research concerns jury decision-making. He is the author of *Common and Uncommon Sense of Social Psychology* (1988) and *Research Methods* (1990) and co-author (with K. Deaux and L. S. Wrightsman) of *Social Psychology in the 90s* (6th edn, 1993).

BRIAN S. EVERITT is Professor of Behavioural Statistics at the Institute of Psychiatry, London. He is the author of *An Introduction to Latent Variable Models* (1984), *Statistical Methods for Medical Investigations* (1989), and *The Analysis of Contingency Tables* (2nd edn, 1992); he is co-author (with G. Dunn) of *Applied Multivariate Data Analysis* (1991). He is currently working on a third edition of his book on *Cluster Analysis*.

ANTHONY GALE is Professor of Psychology at Southampton University, and was president of the British Psychological Society. His research includes physiological studies of information processing and personality, participant observation of family life, and conceptual issues in applied psychology. He has also published critical papers on the teaching of psychology and the failure of psychologists to deploy psychological principles and ethics in the education and treatment of students. He is co-editor (with A. J. Chapman) of *Psychology and Social Problems* (1984) and (with A. Vetere) of *Ecological Studies of Family Life* (1987).

ANTHONY M. GRAZIANO received his PhD in clinical psychology from Purdue University, Indiana, in 1961. He completed a postdoctoral fellowship in child psychology at the Devereux Foundation before joining the faculty at the University of Bridgeport, Connecticut, where he directed several clinical research programmes with severely disturbed children. He has been on the faculty at the State University of New York at Buffalo since 1969, where he has served as the Director of Clinical Training and is the Co-Director of the Research Center for Children and Youth. He has published extensively on psychological treatment of disturbed children and their families and has written seven books, including (as co-author with Michael Raulin) *Research Methods: A Process of Inquiry* (2nd edn, 1993).

A. W. MACRAE   Sandy MacRae is Lecturer in Psychology at the University of Birmingham, where he studies human performance, and sensory psychophysics. He has taught measurement theory, statistics, and research methods to undergraduate and graduate psychologists and to scientists in various industries since 1965. He is a member of UK, US and international (ISO) technical committees concerned with sensory evaluation methods for food and drink.

MICHAEL L. RAULIN received his PhD in clinical psychology from the University of Wisconsin, Madison, in 1977. He joined the faculty of the State University of New York at Buffalo in 1978, where he is currently the Director of Clinical Training and the Administrative Director of the Psychological Services Center. He has published articles on schizophrenia and risk factors for schizophrenia, neurological impact of drug abuse, illusory correlations, and professional development. He is co-author (with Anthony Graziano) of *Research Methods: A Process of Inquiry* (2nd edn, 1993).

DAVID D. STRETCH   After a first degree in psychology from the University College of North Wales (at Bangor), David Stretch completed an MSc in mathematical psychology at Stirling, and a PhD at Birmingham, where he studied the mathematical modelling of memory. He then held a variety of positions at the University of Newcastle upon Tyne and also worked for Newcastle Area Health Authority. In 1986 he joined the Psychiatry Department at Leicester University as a Lecturer in Psychology, specializing in statistical modelling and research design. Because of this expertise, he has been associated with publications in a wide area of psychology; he still manages to continue research into psychometrics, axiomatic measurement theory, and other areas of mathematical psychology.

# SERIES EDITOR'S PREFACE

The *Longman Essential Psychology* series comprises twelve concise and inexpensive paperback volumes covering all of the major topics studied in undergraduate psychology degree courses. The series is intended chiefly for students of psychology and other subjects with psychology components, including medicine, nursing, sociology, social work, and education. Each volume contains five or six accessibly written chapters by acknowledged authorities in their fields, and each chapter includes a list of references and a small number of recommendations for further reading.

Most of the material was prepared originally for the Routledge *Companion Encyclopedia of Psychology* but with a view to later paperback subdivision – the contributors were asked to keep future textbook readers at the front of their minds. Additional material has been added for the paperback series: new co-editors have been recruited for nine of the volumes that deal with highly specialized topics, and each volume has a new introduction, a glossary of technical terms including a number of entries written specially for this edition, and a comprehensive new index.

I am grateful to my literary agents Sheila Watson and Amanda Little for clearing a path through difficult terrain towards the publication of this series, to Sarah Caro of Longman for her patient and efficient preparation of the series, to Brian Parkinson, David Stretch, and Susan Dye for useful advice and comments, and to Carolyn Preston for helping with the compilation of the glossaries.

ANDREW M. COLMAN

# INTRODUCTION

*Andrew M. Colman*
*University of Leicester, England*

Research in psychology or in any other scientific field invariably begins with a question in search of an answer. The question may be purely factual – for example, is sleep-walking more likely to occur during the stage of sleep in which dreams occur, namely rapid eye movement (REM) sleep, than in dreamless (slow-wave) sleep? Alternatively, it may be a practical question – for example, can the use of hypnosis to recover long-forgotten experiences increase the likelihood of false memories? (According to current research findings, incidentally, the answers to these questions are no and yes respectively.) A research question may arise from mere curiosity, from a theory that yields a prediction, or from previous research findings that raise a new question. Whatever its origin, provided that it concerns behaviour or mental experience and that it can be expressed in a suitable form for investigation by empirical methods – that is, by the collection of objective evidence – it is a legitimate question for psychological research.

Psychological research relies on a wide range of methods. This is partly because it is such a diverse discipline, ranging from biological aspects of behaviour to social psychology and from basic research questions to problems that arise in such applied fields as clinical, educational, and industrial or occupational psychology. Most psychological research methods have the ultimate goal of answering empirical questions about behaviour or mental experience through controlled observation. But different questions call for different research methods, because the nature of a question often constrains the methods that can be used to answer it. This volume discusses a wide range of commonly used methods of research and statistical analysis.

The most powerful research method is undoubtedly controlled experimentation. The reason for the unique importance of controlled experiments in psychology is not that they are necessarily any more objective or precise than other methods, but that they are capable of providing firm evidence regarding cause-and-effect relationships, which no other research method can provide. The defining features of the experimental method are manipulation and control. The experimenter manipulates the conjectured causal factor (called the independent variable because it is manipulated independently of other variables) and examines its effects on a suitable measure of the behaviour of interest, called the dependent variable. In multivariate research designs, the interactive effects of several independent variables on two or more dependent variables may be studied simultaneously. In addition to manipulating the independent variable(s) and observing the effects on the dependent variable(s), the experimenter controls all other extraneous variables that might influence the results. Controlled experimentation thus combines the twin features of manipulation (of independent variables) and control (of independent and extraneous variables).

In psychological experiments, extraneous variables can seldom be controlled directly. One reason for this is that people differ from one another in ways that affect their behaviour. Even if these individual differences were all known and understood, they could not be suppressed or held constant while the effects of the independent variable was being examined. This seems to rule out the possibility of experimental control in most areas of psychology, but in the 1920s the British statistician Ronald Aylmer Fisher discovered a remarkable solution to this problem, called randomization.

To understand the idea behind randomization, imagine that the experimenter wishes to test the hypothesis that the anti-depressive drug Prozac (fluoxetine hydrochloride) causes an increase in aggressiveness. The independent variable is ingestion of Prozac and the dependent variable is a score on some suitable test of aggressiveness. The experimenter could assign subjects to two treatment conditions strictly at random, by drawing their names out of a hat, for example, and could then treat the two groups identically apart from the manipulation of the independent variable. Before being tested for aggressiveness, the experimental group could be given a pill containing Prozac and the control group a placebo (an inactive dummy pill). The effect of the randomization would be to control, at a single stroke, for *all* extraneous variables, including ones that the researcher had not even considered. For example, if two-thirds of the subjects were women, then each group would end up roughly two-thirds female, and if some of the subjects had criminal records for offences involving violence, then these people would probably be more or less evenly divided between the experimental and control groups, especially if the groups were large. Randomization would not guarantee that the two groups would be identical but merely that they would tend to be roughly similar on all extraneous variables. More precisely, randomization would ensure that any differences between the groups were distributed strictly according to the laws of chance. Therefore, if the two groups turned out to differ on the test of aggressiveness, this difference would have to be due either to the independent variable (the effect of Prozac) or to chance.

This explains the purpose and function of inferential statistics in psychology. For any specified difference, a statistical test enables a researcher to calculate the probability or odds of a difference as large as that arising by chance alone. In other words, a statistical test tells us the probability of such a large difference arising under the null hypothesis that the independent variable has no effect. If a difference is observed in an experiment, and if the probability under the null hypothesis of such a large difference arising by chance alone is sufficiently small (by convention, usually less than 5 per cent, often written $p < .05$), then the researcher is entitled to conclude with confidence that the observed difference is due to the independent variable. This conclusion can be drawn with confidence, because if the difference is not due to chance, then it *must* be due to the independent variable, provided that the experiment was properly controlled. The logical connection between randomized experimentation and inferential statistics is explained in greater depth in Colman (1988, ch. 4).

A grasp of the elements of statistics is necessary for psychologists, because research findings are generally reported in numerical form and analysed statistically. In some areas of psychology, including naturalistic observations and case-studies (see below), qualitative research methods are occasionally used, and research of this kind requires quite different methods of data collection and analysis. For a survey of the relatively uncommon but none the less important qualitative research methods, including ethnography, personal construct approaches, discourse analysis, and action research, see the book by Banister, Burman, Parker, Taylor and Tindall (1994).

In chapter 1 of this volume, David D. Stretch introduces the fundamental ideas behind experimental design in psychology. He begins by explaining the appropriate form of a psychological research question and how incorrectly formulated questions can sometimes be transformed into questions suitable for experimental investigation. He then discusses experimental control, problems of sampling and randomization, issues of interpretability, plausibility, generalizability, and communicability, and proper planning of research. Stretch concludes his chapter with a discussion of the subtle and complex problems of measurement in psychology. He uses an extremely instructive example to show how two different though equally plausible measures of a dependent variable can lead to completely different − in fact, mutually contradictory − conclusions.

Chapter 2, by Brian S. Everitt, is devoted entirely to analysis of variance designs. These are by far the most common research designs in psychology. Everitt's discussion covers one-way designs, which involve the manipulation of only one independent variable; factorial designs, in which two or more independent variables are manipulated simultaneously; and within-subject repeated-measure designs, in which instead of being randomly assigned to treatment conditions, the same subjects are used in all conditions. Chapter 2 concludes with a discussion of analysis of covariance, a technique designed to increase the sensitivity of analysis of variance by controlling statistically for one or more extraneous variables called covariates. Analysis of covariance is sometimes used in the hope of compensating for the failure to control extraneous variables by randomization, but Everitt discusses certain problems caused by such use.

In chapter 3, A. W. MacRae provides a detailed discussion of the ideas behind statistics, both descriptive and inferential. Descriptive statistics include a variety of methods of summarizing numerical data in ways that make them more easily interpretable, including diagrams, graphs, and numerical summaries such as means (averages), standard deviations (measures of variability), correlations (measures of the degree to which two variables are related to each other), and so forth. Inferential statistical methods are devoted to interpreting data and enabling researchers to decide whether the results of their experiments are statistically significant or may be explained by mere chance. MacRae includes a brief discussion of Bayesian methods, which in contrast to classical statistical methods are designed to answer the more natural question: "How likely is it that such-and-such a conclusion is correct?". For more information on Bayesian methods, the book by Lee (1989) is strongly recommended: it explains the main ideas lucidly without side-stepping difficulties.

Chapter 4, by Michael L. Raulin and Anthony M. Graziano, deals with quasi-experiments and correlational studies. Quasi-experiments, as their name implies, resemble controlled experiments inasmuch as they are intended to answer questions about cause-effect relationships, but they are not strictly experimental because the researcher does not have full control of the conjectured causes or the extraneous variables. Raulin and Graziano discuss several of the most important quasi-experimental research designs used in psychology. Correlational studies are used in situations in which it is either impossible or unethical to manipulate the independent variable(s). In addition, some research questions are concerned not with causal effects but with whether and to what extent two or more variables are related, and in these cases correlational studies are obviously the methods of choice. Raulin and Graziano discuss simple correlations between two variables and more advanced methods, such as simple and multiple linear regression and path analysis.

In chapter 5 of this volume, Francis C. Dane discusses survey methods, naturalistic observations, and case-studies. Surveys, which involve asking representative samples of people standardized questions, are designed to investigate matters of psychological interest in specific sections of a population or in different populations. They usually examine differences between groups defined according to demographic variables such as geographical location, ethnic identity, age, sex, social class, income, marital status, and education. Naturalistic observation, as its name suggests, is a research method used to study naturally occurring behaviour without interacting with the subjects who are being observed.

Case-studies, which Dane discusses only briefly, are detailed investigations of single individuals or occasionally single organizations. In some branches of psychology case-studies are quite common. In abnormal psychology, for example, they usually take the form of detailed descriptions of individuals with unusual or scientifically interesting disorders or responses to new or uncommon treatments. In other areas of psychology case-studies are less common but certainly not non-existent. In the field of cognition, for example, the Russian psychologist Alexander Romanovich Luria spent 30 years studying an individual called Shereshevskii, who was a man with an apparently limitless long-term memory for material of all kinds, including numbers, nonsense syllables, poetry in languages he did not speak, and even elaborate scientific formulas. Luria's (1968) case-study of Shereshevskii is considered a modern classic, and its findings throw light on the nature of short-term and long-term memory. Case-studies also play an important part in the field of cognitive neuropsychology, where researchers examine patterns of normal and abnormal functioning in brain-damaged patients in order to test the validity of competing theories of information processing.

The final chapter, by Anthony Gale, deals with ethical issues in psychological research. The nature of psychology – in particular the fact that its research subjects are people and animals – generates a wide range of ethical problems that, as Gale makes clear, are often far from simple. Ethical guidelines for the conduct of research have been issued by both the American Psychological Association and the British Psychological Society, the two largest professional organizations of psychologists in the world. Gale discusses the content of these codes before focusing on specific areas of concern, including animal experimentation, issues involving informed consent, socially sensitive research, and special problems associated with race and gender.

There are helpful suggestions for further reading at the end of the following chapters. In addition, the full spectrum of psychological research methods is discussed in considerable depth, with numerous real-life examples, by Jones (1995); a wide range of methods is covered more briefly in a multi-authored book edited by Breakwell, Hammond and Fife-Schaw (1995); and a detailed survey of elementary and advanced statistical methods is provided by Boniface (1995).

## REFERENCES

Banister, P., Burman, E., Parker, I., Taylor, M., & Tindall, C. (1994). *Qualitative methods in psychology: A research guide.* Buckingham: Open University Press.

Boniface, D. R. (1995). *Experimental design and statistical methods. For behavioural and social research.* London: Chapman & Hall.

Breakwell, G. M., Hammond, S., & Fife-Schaw, C. (eds). (1995). *Research methods in psychology.* London: Sage.

Colman, A. M. (1988). *What is psychology: The inside story* (2nd edn). London: Routledge.

Jones, J. L. (1995). *Understanding psychological science.* London: HarperCollins.

Lee, P. M. (1989). *Bayesian statistics: An introduction.* London: Edward Arnold.

Luria, A. R. (1968). *The mind of a mnemonist.* New York: Basic Books.

# 1

# EXPERIMENTAL DESIGN

## *David D. Stretch*
### *University of Leicester, England*

Experiments involve
  comparisons
Experimental control and causes
  of behaviour
Populations, samples,
  randomization, and
  representativeness
Interpretability, plausibility,
  generalizability, and
  communicability

Forward planning
Alternative explanations
The methods of measuring and
  the meaning of psychological
  variables
Optimum strategy in
  experimental design
Further reading
References

This chapter deals with experimental design in psychology. Experimental design has a close relationship with statistics and statistical analysis, as it is usually via statistical analysis that we interpret and understand the evidence provided for us by the experiments we carry out. However, statistical analysis is not the only aspect of experimental design that is important, and it is some of these other aspects that will be discussed here.

## EXPERIMENTS INVOLVE COMPARISONS

It is usual that experiments involve comparing conditions, groups of people, or situations on various measures, for example, rather than determining "absolute" values of a single group on one or more measures. So, if we have a theory that states, say, that speech is lateralized in the left hemisphere of the brain in right-handed people, then in order to investigate this hypothesis, we have to frame a research question that involves a comparison of some sort that sheds light on the theory. Similarly, if we have a theory that states that the environmental situation in which people learn information can be used as a cue for later recall of that information, then this needs to be similarly framed as a research question that involves comparisons. Finally, if we consider a theory that rewards and punishments are powerful modifiers of behaviour, we can derive from this theory a research question that asks a comparative question.

To make this clear, the following list of statements can be looked upon as research questions suitable for experimental investigation because they involve comparisons. They may not yet be in a form that can be directly used to frame an experiment, but they are certainly immediate candidates for experimental investigation:

1 Do right-handed people have more difficulty speaking if their left hemisphere is slightly anaesthetized rather than their right hemisphere?
2 Can people remember more information than they otherwise would if they attempt to recall that information in similar environmental situations to those in which it was learned?
3 Does immediate reward of appropriate behaviour in children result in more episodes of appropriate behaviour?

The following are questions that, as they stand, ask about "absolutes". Consequently, they are not immediately available as ready-made research questions that can be investigated by means of experiments.

4 Do people who practise "sleep hygiene" sleep well?
5 Are psychologists closed-minded?

They can, however, be altered so that they do ask about comparisons, though it will be seen that the altered questions are rather different in the kinds of things they are asking about:

4' Does the imposition of a regime of "sleep hygiene" in people who suffer from insomnia cause them to have better quality sleep than they might otherwise experience?
5' Are psychologists more closed-minded than physicists?

Of the two questions 4' and 5', the former more easily allows us to make inferences about potential causes of behaviour than the latter. This is the case even though both pose comparative questions; we shall now discuss the reason for this.

## EXPERIMENTAL CONTROL AND CAUSES OF BEHAVIOUR

The reason why question 5' above does not logically allow statements to be made about the possible cause of any observed differences in behaviour is that the question is asking about the association that exists between pre-existing attributes of people and observable behaviour. As such, then, the study does not exhibit experimental control.

In question 5', the pre-existing attribute is the occupation of the people under study (whether they are psychologists or physicists), and although we could speculate that it was solely being a psychologist or a physicist that caused the observed difference in closed-mindedness, it could equally well be another (unobserved) factor or variable that led them to choose a course in psychology or physics as well as causing them to have particular levels of closed-mindedness.

Question 4', however, involves us causing some change in people who suffer from insomnia (i.e., imposing a regime of sleep hygiene on them), and seeing if a corresponding change in behaviour is observed (i.e., an improved quality of sleep). In these circumstances, we are said to impose a treatment, and so we can have greater confidence in concluding what may have caused the observed difference in behaviour.

Question 4' leads to what is often termed a true experiment whereas question 5' leads to what is known as a correlational study. Now, if it were ethically possible to alter question 5' above, to something like this

5″ Are people who would otherwise possess equal degrees of closed-mindedness affected by the kind of degree course attended so that a psychology course results in *less* closed-mindedness than a physics course?

then this is a research question that would be in a suitable form for a true experiment, because we would essentially be imposing a treatment on people (attendance at either a psychology or physics course), and seeing if this treatment caused a difference in the degree to which they were closed-minded. Of course, issues of plausibility or sensibility and ethical issues would still need to be considered.

The treatments or attributes are usually called independent variables or explanatory variables, whereas the behaviour in which we are attempting to explain the observed differences is usually called the dependent variable or response variable. For complicated experiments, there may be more than one dependent variable, or it may well happen that a variable is both an independent variable and a dependent variable, depending on context. This is particularly prone to happen when investigating proposed networks of causal influences in path analysis (Kenny, 1979), or structural equation modelling (Bollen, 1989; Everitt, 1984; Long, 1983a, 1983b).

Of course, experiments involve more things than are mentioned in the above discussion, but the examples have served to illustrate what is involved in the experimental control of variables. As has been shown, experimental control is quite an important aspect of experiments as it provides a way of identifying or confirming, from all the potential causes of the behaviour under investigation, a sub-set of causes that have a more dominant role in determining the behaviour being studied. If experimental control is particularly good, and our subject-matter for research is particularly well circumscribed, it may well be that we can discover that the total number of potential causes is quite small, but the nature of psychology is such that all behaviour is probably influenced by a very great number of other factors or causes, and so this is not often found to be achievable.

Although experimental control is usually associated with true experiments, this does not mean that it can never be present in any of the other empirical methods. For example, experimental control can be present to a greater or lesser extent in quasi-experiments (Campbell & Stanley, 1966). If case-studies in clinical psychology (say) are designed in a particular way, perhaps by making use of some of the single-case experimental designs mentioned in Barlow and Hersen (1984), experimental control is certainly present. Hence causes of behaviour can potentially be identified from such studies. Similarly, hypothesized networks of causal influences can be investigated in correlational studies by making use of the modelling technique of path analysis (Kenny, 1979), or, for the more adventurous, structural equation modelling or analysis of covariance structures (Bollen, 1989; Everitt, 1984; Long, 1983a, 1983b).

## POPULATIONS, SAMPLES, RANDOMIZATION, AND REPRESENTATIVENESS

There is another feature of experiments that should also be mentioned at this stage: randomization. This term is more usually associated with statistics, but it is necessary to mention it here as there are issues that are tackled when designing an experiment that are most effectively explained by using concepts commonly employed within statistics. Closely bound to the idea of randomization are the ideas of populations, samples, and representativeness, and it is difficult to explain randomization without also using the latter three terms.

A population is the entire set of things about which we hope the experiment will allow us to make inferential statements. Thus, if we want to investigate degrees of closed-mindedness among psychologists, the population is the entire set of psychologists. (Although logically this should also include all psychologists who have ever lived, and are yet to live and become psychologists, it is almost always impractical to include literally everyone when planning and designing our experiments.) Similarly, if we want to investigate whether the aromas of lemon and pine can reduce the number of keyboard errors committed by people when working at a computer, then the population consists of all work sessions when people are using a computer keyboard.

We do not usually have the time to observe all elements of a population, and so we arrange to observe only a sample. If we choose random samples, using a suitable randomization technique, then we have some confidence that we can extrapolate or generalize the results we find from studying the sample to the entire population. Selecting a random sample is a very good way of ensuring that the sample is representative of the entire population of interest; consequently we can have confidence in being able to extrapolate or generalise any results based on this random sample. We shall see (below) that generalizability has been identified as being of high importance in psychological research, and so it is clear that random samples and representativeness need to be considered carefully. A random sample from a population can be constructed by ensuring that every member of the population has an equal chance of being picked as a member of the sample.

Constructing a random sample is often very difficult to arrange, but it is a worthwhile goal to achieve. The issue of representativeness has already been mentioned. Another benefit, arguably the greatest, of using an appropriate randomization technique concerns the random assignment of subjects to one or more experimental groups or conditions. This results in the subsequent experimental control of all ways in which the groups could differ, other than the ways the experimenter imposes by manipulation of the independent variable.

So, if we take our random sample, and then assign its units (usually subjects) to the experimental groups or conditions so that the final sizes of the experimental groups are equal, we will, on average, control every possible way in which the experimental groups could differ in terms of pre-existing attributes. This will, of course, not include the difference we are investigating in the experiment, which is not an attribute, but an imposed treatment. The principle of randomization was first expounded by the statistician Ronald A. Fisher in 1926 and popularized by his later textbook (Fisher, 1966); the principle proves to be one of the crucial aspects of true experiments. Note that the experimental groups ideally must be of the same size in order for this result or property of randomization to hold. Thus, if groups are unequal in size, either through poor planning, or subject attrition or drop-out (i.e., subjects failing for any reason to complete the experiment, resulting in groups of different size), then alternative explanations of any differences among the experimental groups may become viable; these alternative explanations will hinge on the different compositions of the groups, based on other, unmeasured features or attributes of the subjects. Furthermore, the more unequal the sizes of the experimental groups, the greater is the chance that alternative explanations become viable, and indeed they may become the most plausible explanation of an experiment's results.

It is therefore clear that if one wants to keep to a minimum the possibility that alternative explanations can explain the results of one's experiments, then ensuring that the experimental groups are of the same size is a useful first step to take. Furthermore, if subject attrition or drop-out occurs, it is useful to see if the remaining experimental groups differ in some attribute or attributes of the subjects. If they do, an alternative explanation of any differences among the groups may be possible in which the differences are explained in terms of the attribute differences among the experimental groups.

Even if the groups are of equal size, though, there is still a chance that the experimental groups will differ in some pre-existing attribute, because the principle of randomization will work only in the long run. In order to rule out these kinds of alternative explanations, sometimes extensive numbers of additional subject attributes will have to be measured, and this becomes very time-consuming. Consequently, ensuring equally sized groups and minimizing subject attrition are advisable in true experiments. Furthermore, if there is a suspicion that the groups are likely to differ on any pre-existing attribute that could form the basis of a plausible alternative explanation, then, even if the groups are of equal size, measurements of the attributes identified and their incorporation into any subsequent statistical analysis (such as analysis of covariance, and suchlike) will often help.

To illustrate some problems of random sampling, suppose we want to investigate by experiment whether people are better able to write down an address if a radio announcer reads out the complete address a number of times, or whether it is better for each line to be read out a number of times before the announcer moves on to the next line of address. (That is, if the lines of addresses are represented by the letters ABCD, the first method would correspond to people hearing ABCDABCDABCD, whereas the second method would correspond to AAABBBCCCDDD.) In the UK, the BBC usually has its announcers reading out entire addresses a number of times, but there was a short period when announcers repeated each line a number of times before moving on to the next line.

Now, we could ask for volunteers who would participate in this experiment. However, we would not then be constructing a strictly random sample, as the people who are unwilling to come forward and volunteer would never be picked. And, because some people would never be picked as members of the sample, our sample is at great risk of not being representative of everybody because it may contain a disproportionate number of people who share or possess a particular attribute. In this example, it could be that people who tend to volunteer are those who have found the current method of reading out addresses on the radio very difficult to follow, and so may be better able to write the addresses down if the second method of delivery was employed. One explanation of how this may have come about might be that they are rather irritated by the current method of reading out addresses, and may therefore have a slightly greater inclination to volunteer for the study. If such people were more prone to volunteer, then the resulting sample would not be representative of the entire population we originally wanted to generalize our results to, and any such generalization would consequently be subject to bias.

Given that we are ethically obliged to avoid deception of subjects who participate in experiments, a great deal of psychological research could be biased in a way similar to the above example. The reason is that we cannot be sure that we can justifiably generalize from our sample to the entire population because of sampling bias. The situation could be retrieved somewhat by narrowing the population to which we generalize, so that our sample would be more representative (Coombs, 1983, 1984). Another way of tackling this potential problem would be to change the way in which the sample is drawn up and constructed so that it is more representative of the original population of interest. Finally, we could leave the design unchanged, but exercise great care and caution in generalizing the results.

## INTERPRETABILITY, PLAUSIBILITY, GENERALIZABILITY, AND COMMUNICABILITY

Now is a suitable point at which to introduce four key features of any experiment (or, indeed, any other type of psychological research). The four most important features are those of interpretability, plausibility, generalizability, and communicability.

First, we must design experiments whose results we can easily interpret. One way of improving the interpretability of an experiment is to strive towards simplicity and clarity without descending into triviality. This can be very difficult to attain as Nature does not usually work in a simple manner. However, one should not overcomplicate experiments by, for example, collecting additional observations because they "could" be useful in an as-yet unspecified manner. A simple, clear research question, with an experiment closely focused on answering just that simple, clear question is best. Furthermore, a great help in attaining interpretability is to design experiments in which all alternative explanations of the results, apart from the one relevant to the research question, are eliminated. This subsidiary goal is discussed further below.

Second, an experiment must be designed so as to be a plausible way of investigating the research question. Similarly, the explanations that emerge from the results should also be plausible. Once again, simplicity, clarity, and closely focused research are likely to succeed in attaining plausibility, as well as attention to the elimination of alternative explanations.

Third, we must ensure that the results of the experiment are generalizable in the way we want: we need to be able to state with justification that the conclusions to which we come, based on the sample we used in the experiment, apply to the population from which the sample was drawn.

Finally, since psychological research is really part of a collective effort, we need to be able to communicate our results and conclusions effectively to our fellow researchers. Once again, simplicity, clarity, and closely focused research will facilitate communicability.

7

The above points have been introduced by Levy (1981). The message can best be summed up with the following sentence:

*Keep things as simple, clear, and focused as possible, because they will always turn out to be more complicated than you imagine.*

There are a number of strategies that can be adopted to ensure that experiments have the features mentioned above, and one of these (constructing a representative sample of the population of interest) has already been mentioned. A strategy that underlies most of the others, though, is forward planning.

## FORWARD PLANNING

To maximize our chances of completing experiments that possess the characteristics introduced above, a period of extremely careful planning preceding any collection of observations is often helpful. This forward planning will be easier to accomplish if we consider a number of subsidiary goals along the way (mentioned below). The advisability of planning is so important that its message can be summed up simply:

*If you fail to plan, you are planning to fail.*

Informal evidence from my colleagues who also give research advice to people shows that inadequate planning occurs frequently. As Levy (1981) notes, failure to plan leads to situations where researchers have collected uninterpretable observations and data. Additionally, the sample used may not be representative of the population about which inferences are to be made. Often, the researcher consults someone who has expertise in research design or statistical analysis only after the observations have been gathered – and this is too late. Usually, a large amount of time and effort will be involved in rescuing an inadequately planned experiment, and this rescue bid is not bound to succeed. In these circumstances, the only advice that ought to be given to the researcher is to throw away the observations and start again properly – making sure that sufficient forward planning is carried out before any move is made to gather observations. Careful forward planning can drastically reduce the resulting waste of time and resources. Hand & Everitt (1987a), Greenfield (1987), and Barnett (1987) (all contained in Hand & Everitt, 1987b) discuss this issue from the point of view of statisticians.

Finally, too much emphasis is placed on checking that the data emerging from an experiment can be (statistically) analysed. The conditions that determine whether a statistical test can be justifiably applied to a set of data do not necessarily include or require that the data are appropriate for the substantive psychological research question: this issue is assumed to have been dealt with beforehand in the forward planning stage. It is much more important to determine that the experiment is interpretable (Levy, 1981). Although Kenny (1979) was writing about path analysis and causal modelling, a sentence of his, with a minor addition, is very relevant here: "Good ideas do not come out of computer packages [or statistical tests], but from people's heads" (p. 8). Instead, the planning needs to concentrate on maximizing the interpretability, plausibility, generalizability, and communicability of the experiment, because if they are maximized, it is almost always the case that the resulting data can be statistically analysed.

## ALTERNATIVE EXPLANATIONS

If we tackle a number of subsidiary issues or goals in the forward planning stage, it becomes easier to design experiments that attain the four goals of interpretability, plausibility, generalizability, and communicability. One of these subsidiary issues is that we must eliminate, as far as possible, any alternative explanations of the results we could obtain. So, the research must be designed in such a way that, when any necessary statistical analyses have been completed, an interpretation of the results remains that makes use of only those explanations of relevance to the original research question.

From what has been written earlier about experimental control, it should be obvious that a good way of minimizing the chance of alternative explanations being offered for experimental results is to use experimental control of variables, and hence design and carry out "true experiments". (Note, however, that there are alternative points of view to the one offered here, some of which are discussed in Bickhard, 1992.) Furthermore, if sampling is done with care, possible alternative explanations which rely on the samples used being unrepresentative of the population of interest cannot be proposed. (This issue was discussed above.) Coombs talks about a decision having to be made about "saying more about less, or less about more" (Coombs, 1983, 1984), and this is clearly related to the matter under discussion here.

It is important to become skilled at identifying the potential alternative explanations for results of experiments, because, once identified, the design of the experiments can be modified to try to eliminate them. This must be done in the planning stage, otherwise much time and effort is wasted in carrying out and completing flawed research. Huck and Sandler (1979) devote an entire book to giving examples of psychological research where the reader is invited to identify, with justifications, alternative explanations for the results the researchers report.

The following example comes from their book. The Pepsi-Cola Company carried out research to determine whether people tended to prefer Pepsi Cola to Coca Cola. Participants were asked to taste and then state which of two glasses of cola they preferred. The two glasses were not labelled "Pepsi" or "Coke" for obvious reasons. Instead, the Coke glass was labelled $Q$ and the Pepsi glass was labelled $M$. The results showed that "more than half chose Pepsi over Coke" (Huck & Sandler, 1979, p. 11). Are there any explanations for this difference other than the taste of the two drinks? One alternative explanation mentioned was the systematic bias that was introduced into the study by always using letter $Q$ for Coke and $M$ for Pepsi. When the Coca Cola Company conducted another study where Coke was put into *both* glasses, one labelled $M$ and the other $Q$, the results showed that a majority of people chose the glass labelled $M$ in preference to the glass labelled $Q$. Since the taste of cola in the two glasses was presumably the same in this second study, the original conclusion (people prefer Pepsi to Coke) could not be upheld, and another alternative explanation of the results, based on letter preferences, could be offered instead. (Of course, there are still more alternative interpretations – for example, did people always taste the cola in glass $M$ before the cola in glass $Q$? If so, would this affect the results?)

Possible alternative explanations of an experiment's results, like the above example, should be considered at the planning stage, and if they exist and are important, the design of the experiment should be changed to rule them out. It may not always be possible to do this, but, even so, the attempt should be made.

Consider another example, not directly taken from Huck and Sandler (1979). Suppose we want to determine whether taking a particular drug affects people's reaction times. To investigate this, we might take a large number of people and assign each person to one of two groups at random. Both groups would then complete a simple reaction time task so that we could derive a typical score on that task for each person. In one group we would administer the drug in tablet form, and in the other group we would administer a placebo, which in this case would be a tablet, identical to the tablet in the first group, except that it would not contain the drug. If the resulting statistical analysis of the reaction times showed a difference in the typical scores of the two groups (for example, if the drug group overall had shorter reaction times than the placebo group), we could conclude that the difference between the two groups in the design (drug vs no drug) *caused* the difference in the typical scores.

It may be possible to identify alternative explanations that would explain the results. Most of these alternative explanations would not explain the difference in the reaction times in terms of the drug, but would rely on the discovery of other ways in which the two groups differ. This is obviously an issue to do with random sampling and representativeness (discussed above), and using those ideas would ensure that the two groups were unlikely to differ in any characteristic other than whether they were given a drug or a placebo. If alternative explanations are easy to discover, and they take the form of discovering further ways in which the two groups differ, then this may indicate that not enough care was taken in randomly allocating the people to the two groups. This would be another example of insufficient forward planning.

In particular, note that if we assigned people to the drug and the placebo groups not at random, but according to whether they were already taking the drug in question or not, then the taking of the drug or the placebo would no longer be a treatment applied to each person, but would rather be an attribute of each person. Consequently, there could quite likely be many ways in which the two groups differed other than the mere taking of the drug or not; for example, the group of people taking the drug could already have a particular illness. Alternative explanations could be offered that explained any difference in reaction times in terms of whether the people had these illnesses or not rather than whether they were taking the drug or the placebo.

There are a number of standard experimental designs that can be used to control variables and, at the same time, determine whether possible alternative explanations can be ruled out. Details of some of these can be found in Spector (1981). Additionally, there is an entire class of statistical analyses, known as analysis of variance, that has been developed to allow various kinds of alternative explanations to be ruled out at the same time as providing a coherent and consistent approach to statistical analysis (as long as certain assumptions can be made about independence of scores from each other, and the way random error can affect these scores). Good sources for these kinds of approaches are Fleiss (1986), Myers (1979), and Pedhazur and Schmelkin (1991).

## THE METHODS OF MEASURING AND THE MEANING OF PSYCHOLOGICAL VARIABLES

Another subsidiary goal that must be considered is the careful examination of the meaning and the method of measurement of the psychological variables relevant to the experiment. If this is not done, we may find that the measures we use are very different (in a way that has not been clearly justified) from other similar experiments, thus making the integration of different experiments in the same research area very difficult. However, a more serious problem is that another experiment, identical to the first apart from the particular way of measuring the psychological variables, may yield quite different results, and it is important to know to what extent the results obtained reflect the particular method of measuring things, rather than the way in which the underlying psychological processes work. These kinds of issues are often labelled "methodological problems" in psychology, but they are almost always substantive psychological issues in their own right. Consequently, they are worthy of being researched in their own right, rather than being treated as mere annoyances. In fact, most of the "problems" of psychological measurement mentioned here are researched within psychology quite extensively. However, the research (some of which is known as *Axiomatic Measurement Theory*) can be highly mathematical in nature and is therefore not easily accessible to many psychologists. For those who wish to see some of this material, Krantz, Luce, Suppes, and Tversky (1971), Luce, Krantz, Suppes, and Tversky (1990), and Suppes, Krantz, Luce, and Tversky (1989) are the main sources. More accessible sources are Falmagne

(1985), French (1981), Levelt, Riemersma, and Bunt (1972), and van der Ven (1980, chap. 10).

The meaning of psychological terms, and hence the measurement of them, is a particular problem in psychology because psychologists sometimes have no widely agreed method of measuring psychological concepts like depression, intelligence, pain, performance, memory, or learning. The usual tactic used in psychology to overcome this problem is to make use of operational definitions. A definition of a psychological construct is an operational definition if it consists of a description of the operations that are performed to measure the psychological construct. So, in an experiment investigating speed of information processing, performance may be operationally defined as the reaction times people have to certain stimuli. Similarly, the degree of depression may be operationally defined to be the scores that people obtain when they complete a depression questionnaire.

There is obviously a problem with these kinds of definitions if they are used in an unthinking way, because the definitions are entirely circular. A psychological construct is defined in terms of the operations necessary to measure it, and the measurements are defined to be measures of the psychological construct! In fact, the originator of operational definitions (Percy Bridgman, a physicist) never intended them to be the *sole* definitions offered for a construct, and details of the history of operational definitions are available in a number of sources (Bickhard, 1992; Green, 1992; Koch, 1992). However, we are left with a problem of what to do if we can no longer use operational definitions to help us define psychological constructs. Psychologists may sometimes not make sufficient use of good dictionaries, constructed by lexicographers, as a means to help them determine the "standard" meaning of some constructs, although this does not always provide a satisfactory solution. A useful rule of thumb is to consider many different ways of measuring the psychological construct of interest and determine the extent to which each method could yield different experimental results. If you find that the measurement techniques radically affect the results that emerge, this should indicate that more work is needed on developing the underlying psychological and measurement models to explain these effects. Axiomatic measurement theory (mentioned above) is potentially useful here, though most researchers would find it difficult to work with. Concentration on the purpose and the meaning of the measurements often helps.

For example, in measuring change in psychological variables, a simple way of assessing changes is to take the straightforward difference between scores obtained on repeated administration of the same instrument as a measure of change, but this can sometimes lead to difficulties that are conceptual rather than statistical. If we take simple difference scores, we are assuming that we are measuring the same psychological attributes, but if the measures are of something that is subject to developmental processes this may not be justifiable. If we administered a simple addition and subtraction test to 5-year-old children, and then administered the same test to the children when they were 16, the first score is likely to measure the extent to which the children have acquired the skills of addition and subtraction, whereas the second score may be more likely to measure the efficiency with which the children can apply the already-acquired skills of addition and subtraction. Depending on what one wanted to do, the simple difference score approach could be appropriate or inappropriate. This matter is discussed in Plewis (1985), who gives alternative methods of analysing data from such studies, as does Goldstein (1979).

However, the most striking example of the problem of ambiguous psychological terms is best left to the end. This example clearly shows the necessity of careful thought and analysis of experiments. The possible solutions will not be easy for most psychologists to grapple with, but in order to build a solid and plausible set of psychological sciences, they must be confronted. Possible means of dealing with these issues are either purely statistical, or involve the use of axiomatic measurement theory ideas. However, greater mathematical and statistical understanding and expertise will be required for psychologists to master and hence make proper use of these techniques.

If one wishes to determine, for right-handed people, in which hemisphere speech is lateralized, one could get people to balance a rod vertically on the end of the index finger. Subjects would do this separately for right and left hands when either speaking or silent. The time taken from the start of balancing each rod until it fell from the finger would be observed. Thus we would take observations from people balancing rods in four different situations: balancing in the right hand when silent, balancing in the right hand when speaking, balancing in the left hand when silent, and balancing in the left hand when speaking. A graph which might be typically obtained of mean performance in the $2 \times 2 = 4$ experimental conditions is shown in Figure 1: better performance for balancing with right hands rather than left hands; better performance when silent rather than speaking; and a greater difference between silent and speaking performance in the right-handed than the left-handed condition.

Because there is contralateral control of movement by the two hemispheres of the brain, right-handed balancing is controlled by the left hemisphere, and left-handed balancing is controlled by the right hemisphere. Given that the disadvantage of speaking compared with being silent is greater when balancing with the right hand rather than the left hand, this suggests that speech is lateralized in the left hemisphere. This conclusion relies on the assumption that it is usually more difficult for a hemisphere to control two things at the same time rather than one. (For more details of experiments like this one, see Hicks, 1975; Kinsbourne and Cook, 1971.)

However, the data for performance need not be analysed as a time-based measure of mean seconds per rod, as in Figure 1. Instead, a speed-based measure of rods per second can be derived from the same observations by taking the reciprocal of the performance points shown in Figure 1. No change

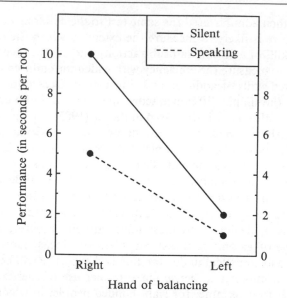

*Figure 1*  Graph showing hypothetical results from the rod-balancing experiment using a time-based measure of performance. This shows an interaction between hand of balancing and the speaking and silent conditions that would lead one to conclude that speech was lateralized in the left hemisphere
*Source*: Results based on work by Kinsbourne and Cook, 1971, and Hicks, 1975

to the treatment of the observations or of the interpretation of the results occurs other than this re-scaling of the dependent variable. Figure 2 shows the identical observations re-scaled in this way.

This figure shows that the nature of the interaction has been reversed by this simple re-scaling of the observations. Using the same arguments and assumptions that were used to interpret Figure 1, we can interpret Figure 2 as follows: better performance for balancing with right hands rather than left hands; better performance when silent rather than speaking; and a greater difference between silent and speaking performance in the left-handed than the right-handed condition. (Note that the re-scaling is such that low scores indicate better performance than high scores when performance is measured in rods per second.) Given that the disadvantage of speaking compared with being silent is greater when balancing with the left hand rather than the right hand, this suggests that speech is lateralized in the right hemisphere. This conclusion also relies on the assumption that it is usually more difficult for a hemisphere to control two things at the same time rather than one.

So, by re-scaling the observations, quite legitimately, from a time-based measure to a speed-based measure and by using exactly the same assumptions to interpret the resulting graph, we come to opposite conclusions about the hemisphere in which speech is lateralized. Unless there are very good grounds

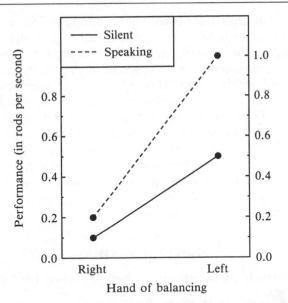

*Figure 2* Graph showing hypothetical results from the rod-balancing experiment using a speed-based measure of performance derived from the identical observations used in Figure 1. This shows an interaction between hand of balancing and the speaking and silent conditions that would lead one to conclude that speech was lateralized in the right hemisphere
*Source*: Results based on work by Kinsbourne and Cook, 1971, and Hicks, 1975

for choosing one form of measure over another, any monotonic transform of the dependent variable can be justified. So, results like those shown above cannot allow us to decide with certainty in which hemisphere speech is lateralized. In this case, there are alternative sources of evidence that allow us to decide in which hemisphere of the brain speech is lateralized, but in many cases within psychology this will not be the case. It should be clear that a greater emphasis on the meaning, method, and understanding of the psychological measurements one is making is required. And to do this, greater expertise among psychologists of the ideas explored in axiomatic approaches to psychological measurement is needed.

## OPTIMUM STRATEGY IN EXPERIMENTAL DESIGN

Many issues have been mentioned that need to be considered when designing experiments. These issues have to be thought about and decisions made *before* the collection of observations begins. It may be difficult to remember all the issues, and so the following strategy may help ensure that any flaws in a planned experiment have a good chance of being detected before observations have been gathered.

If the proposed experiment is written up during the planning stage, as if the research has already been completed, it will help to highlight any areas that may need further consideration. This will often be helped if, in the results section, a number of alternative sets of dummy results that could plausibly be obtained are described. Thus, the issues of interpretability, plausibility, generalizability, and communicability will be considered in the planning stage. Furthermore, by considering a number of plausible sets of results, attention is placed upon possible alternative explanations.

A useful side-effect of this strategy is that the actual paper or final report is largely written by the time the observations have been collected. Thus, the phase of research that is often seen as the most tedious − writing up after the analysis has been completed, often under time pressure − will have its undesirable qualities reduced somewhat.

## FURTHER READING

Coombs, C. H. (1983). *Psychology and mathematics*. Ann Arbor, MI: University of Michigan Press.

Huck, S. W., & Sandler, H. M. (1979). *Rival hypotheses: Alternative interpretations of data based conclusions*. New York: Harper & Row.

Kenny, D. A. (1979). *Correlation and causality*. New York: Wiley.

Levy, P. (1981). On the relation between method and substance in psychology. *Bulletin of the British Psychological Society, 34*, 265–270.

van der Ven, A. H. G. S. (1980). *Introduction to scaling*. Chichester: Wiley.

## REFERENCES

Barlow, D. H., & Hersen, M. (1984). *Single case experimental designs: Strategies for studying behavior change* (2nd edn). New York: Pergamon.

Barnett, V. (1987). Straight consulting. In D. J. Hand & B. S. Everitt (Eds) *The statistical consultant in action* (chap. 3, pp. 26–41). Cambridge: Cambridge University Press.

Bickhard, M. H. (1992). Myths of science. *Theory and Psychology, 2*(3), 321–337.

Bollen, K. A. (1989). *Structural equations with latent variables*. New York: Wiley.

Campbell, D. T., & Stanley, J. C. (1966). *Experimental and quasi-experimental designs for research*. Chicago, IL: Rand McNally.

Combs, C. H. (1983). *Psychology and mathematics*. Ann Arbor, MI: University of Michigan Press.

Combs, C. H. (1984). *Theory and experiment in psychology* (transcript of talk presented to the European Mathematical Psychology Group, 29 March 1983, at the University of Hamburg, FRG).

Everitt, B. S. (1984). *An introduction to latent variable models*. London: Chapman & Hall.

Falmagne, J.-C. (1985). *Elements of psychophysical theory*. Oxford: Clarendon.

Fisher, R. A. (1926). The arrangement of field experiments. *Journal of the Ministry of Agriculture, 33*, 503–513.

Fisher, R. A. (1966). *The design of experiments* (8th edn). London: Oliver & Boyd (1st edn published 1938).

Fleiss, J. L. (1986). *The design and analysis of clinical experiments*. New York: Wiley.

French, S. (1981). Measurement theory and examinations. *British Journal of Mathematical and Statistical Psychology, 34*, 38–49.

Goldstein, H. (1979). *The design and analysis of longitudinal studies: Their role in the measurement of change*. London: Academic Press.

Green, C. D. (1992). Of immortal mythological beasts. *Theory and Psychology, 2*(3), 291–320.

Greenfield, T. (1987). Consultants' cameos: A chapter of encounters. In D. J. Hand & B. S. Everitt (Eds) *The statistical consultant in action* (chap. 2, pp. 11–25). Cambridge: Cambridge University Press.

Hand, D. J., & Everitt, B. S. (1987a). Statistical consultancy. In D. J. Hand & B. S. Everitt (Eds) *The statistical consultant in action* (chap. 1, pp. 1–10). Cambridge: Cambridge University Press.

Hand, D. J., & Everitt, B. S. (1987b). *The statistical consultant in action*. Cambridge: Cambridge University Press.

Hicks, R. E. (1975). Intrahemispheric response competition between vocal and unimanual performance in normal adult human males. *Journal of Comparative and Physiological Psychology, 89*(1), 50–60.

Huck, S. W., & Sandler, H. M. (1979). *Rival hypotheses: Alternative interpretations of data based conclusions*. New York: Harper & Row.

Kenny, D. A. (1979). *Correlation and causality*. New York: Wiley.

Kinsbourne, M., & Cook, J. (1971). Generalized and lateralized effects of concurrent verbalization on a unimanual skill. *Quarterly Journal of Experimental Psychology, 23*, 341–345.

Koch, S. (1992). Psychology's Bridgman *vs*. Bridgman's Bridgman. *Theory and Psychology, 2*(3), 261–290.

Krantz, D. H., Luce, R. D., Suppes, P., & Tversky, A. (1971). *Additive and polynomial representations* (vol. 1 of *Foundations of measurement*). New York: Academic Press.

Levelt, W. J., Riemersma, J. B., & Bunt, A. A. (1972). Binaural additivity of loudness. *British Journal of Mathematical and Statistical Psychology, 25*, 51–68.

Levy, P. (1981). On the relation between method and substance in psychology. *Bulletin of the British Psychological Society, 34*, 265–270.

Long, J. S. (1983a). *Confirmatory factor analysis*. Beverly Hills, CA: Sage.

Long, J. S. (1983b). *Covariance structure models: An introduction to LISREL*. Beverly Hills, CA: Sage.

Luce, R. D., Krantz, D. H., Suppes, P., & Tversky, A. (1990). *Representation, axiomatization, and invariance* (vol. 3 of *Foundations of measurement*). San Diego, CA: Academic Press.

Myers, J. L. (1979). *Fundamentals of experimental design* (3rd edn). Boston, MA: Allyn & Bacon.

Pedhazur, E. J., & Schmelkin, L. P. (1991). *Measurement, design and analysis: an integrated approach*. Hillsdale, NJ: Lawrence Erlbaum.

Plewis, I. (1985). *Analyzing change*. Chichester: Wiley.

Spector, P. E. (1981). *Research designs*. Beverly Hills, CA: Sage.

Suppes, P., Krantz, D. H., Luce, R. D., & Tversky, A. (1989). *Geometrical, threshold, and probabilistic representations* (vol. 2 of *Foundations of measurement*). San Diego, CA: Academic Press.

van der Ven, A. H. G. S. (1980). *Introduction to scaling*. Chichester: Wiley.

# 2

# ANALYSIS OF VARIANCE DESIGNS

## Brian S. Everitt

### University of London Institute of Psychiatry, England

It is said that when Gertrude Stein lay dying, she roused briefly and asked her assembled friends, "Well, what's the answer?" They remained uncomfortably quiet at which she sighed, "in that case, what's the question?"

Research in psychology, and in science in general, is about searching for the answers to particular questions of interest. Do politicians have higher IQ scores than academics? Do men have faster reaction times than women? Should phobic patients be treated by psychotherapy or by a behavioural treatment such as flooding? Do children who are abused have more problems later in life than children who are not abused? Do children of divorced parents suffer more marital breakdowns themselves than children from more stable family backgrounds? Other questions, for example "Does God exist?" and "Is marriage bad?" are, however, *not* the province of the research psychologist or of science in general. Why not? Why are such questions fundamentally different from the kind listed earlier.

The acid test by which scientific questions may be divided from the non-scientific is that the former must be falsifiable, that is, capable in principle of being proved false by scientific investigation. From the scientists' point of view, the strongest theories are those which allow the most opportunities to falsify them, but which withstand all such attempts. In science, this does not mean that a particular theory or hypothesis has been confirmed: hypotheses can never be proved to be true however much the current weight of evidence is in their favour (consider, for example, Newton's theory of gravitation); they can only be shown to be worth retaining and perhaps subjecting to further and more rigorous testing.

Having decided that a question is scientific, however, does not necessarily mean that its investigation will be straightforward. Careful planning will almost certainly be required, using well-established principles from the statistical theory of design. Statistical primarily because of the inherent variability in observations on human and animal subjects. Consider the question "Do British politicians have higher IQs than British academics?" Suppose ten politicians allow their IQs to be measured (this is after all a hypothetical example!), and similarly ten academics, with the results shown in Table 1. Clearly some politicians have higher scores than some academics and vice versa. But what about the difference in average or mean IQ in the two groups? From Table 1 it is seen that for these two particular sets of samples the average IQ of academics is higher than that of politicians. But if we took further samples would this always be so? Can anything be concluded about the difference in average IQ of all British politicians and all British academics from the result found in this particular sample? Drawing conclusions about a population on the basis of observations on a sample of values is the role of inferential statistics.

In any serious study of the IQs of politicians and academics, of course, many other aspects of the design would need to be considered. For example, should only people of the same sex be considered? Or only politicians of a particular party? Or only academics from a particular discipline? And should

*Table 1* IQ scores of samples of British academics and politicians

|  | Academics | Politicians |
| --- | --- | --- |
|  | 106 | 110 |
|  | 99 | 112 |
|  | 122 | 115 |
|  | 128 | 105 |
|  | 105 | 128 |
|  | 107 | 127 |
|  | 131 | 109 |
|  | 119 | 99 |
|  | 99 | 110 |
|  | 132 | 104 |
| Mean | 114.80 | 111.90 |
| SD | 13.06 | 9.36 |

19

age be taken into account? Perhaps even more fundamental are considerations of the IQ measurements involved, are they, for example, reliable and valid?

## MEASUREMENT

Measurement taken during scientific investigations should be objective, precise, and reproducible. Clearly not all measurement is the same. Measuring an individual's weight is qualitatively different from measuring his or her response to some treatment in terms such as "improved" or "not improved". Measurement scales are differentiated according to the degree of precision in the measurement. The comment that a woman is tall is not as accurate as specifying that her height is 1.88 metres. Certain characteristics of interest are more amenable to precise measurement than others. Given an accurate thermometer, an individual's temperature can be measured very precisely. Quantifying the level of anxiety or depression of patients, or assessing their degree of pain, are, however, far more difficult measurement tasks. Measurement scales may be classified into a hierarchy ranging from categorical through ordinal to interval and finally ratio scales. Details of the characteristics of each type of scale are given in Everitt (1989).

An important component of many scientific investigations is the assessment of the reliability and consideration of the validity of the measurements to be made. In very general terms, reliability concerns the variability in repeated measurements made on the same material by the same measuring instrument, and validity expresses the extent to which a measuring instrument measures the characteristic it purports to measure. (Both terms are explained in more detail in Schontz, 1986.) But one characteristic of many behavioural and social measurements that distinguishes them from physical measurements is that they are obtained from the responses to several different questions or test items. The weight of an object is given by a single instrument reading whereas an intelligence quotient may be calculated from answers given to 50 or 100 individual tests (items) of cognitive ability. For such measures the reliability of the total test score is estimated using the subtotals obtained from splitting the test into two equal sized groups of comparable items. The result is what is generally known as the *split-half reliability*. (For details see Dunn, 1989.)

In many areas of research the observer, interviewer, or rater is an obvious source of measurement error, and reliability studies are often required to investigate the measurement procedures to be used for collecting the data of interest. Details of how such studies should be conducted are given in Dunn (1989). That such studies are crucial is emphasized by the following quotation from Fleiss (1986).

The most elegant design of a study will not overcome the damage caused by unreliable or imprecise measurement. The requirement that one's data be of high quality is at least an important component of a proper study design as the requirement for randomization, double blinding, controlling where necessary for prognostic factors, and so on. Larger sample sizes than otherwise necessary, biased estimates, and even biased samples are some of the untoward consequences of unreliable measurements that can be demonstrated. (p. 1)

## OBSERVATIONAL AND EXPERIMENTAL STUDIES

Research studies can be divided roughly into those that are observational and those that are experimental. Both generally involve the comparison of two (or more) groups of subjects, one group which has received the new treatment or been exposed to a particular risk factor or whatever, and another group which has received only the normal treatment as a placebo or has not been exposed to the risk factor. (Studies in which, for example, all patients are given a new treatment are generally neither scientifically nor ethically acceptable.) The basic differences between the two types of studies is the amount of control which the investigator has over the way in which the groups of subjects to be compared are constructed. In an observational study there is essentially no control and in an experimental study usually complete control, although there are types of studies which fall somewhere between these two extremes (see below). In an investigation into the relationship between smoking and systolic blood pressure, for example, the researcher cannot allocate subjects to be smokers and non-smokers; instead the systolic blood pressure of naturally occurring groups of individuals who smoke and those who do not would be compared. In such a study any difference found between the blood pressure of the two groups would be open to three possible explanations.

1 Smoking causes a change in systolic blood pressure.
2 Level of blood pressure has a tendency to encourage or discourage smoking.
3 Some unidentified factors play a part in determining both the level of blood pressure and whether or not a person smokes.

In contrast, in an experimental study, investigators may allocate subjects to groups in a way of their choosing. For example, in a comparison of a new treatment with one used previously, the researcher would have complete control over which subjects received which treatment. The manner in which this control is exercised is, of course, crucial to the acceptability or otherwise of the study. If, for example, subjects who are first to volunteer are all allocated to the new treatment, then the two groups may differ in level of motivation and so subsequently in performance. Observed treatment differences would be confounded with differences produced by the allocation procedure.

The method most often used to overcome such problems is random allocation of subjects to treatments. Whether a subject receives the new or the old treatment is decided, for example, by the toss of a coin. The primary benefit that randomization has is the chance (and therefore impartial) assignment of extraneous influences among the groups to be compared and it offers this control over such influences whether or not they are known by the experimenter to exist. Note that randomization does not claim to render the two samples equal with regard to these influences. If, however, the same procedure were applied in repeated samplings, equality would be achieved in the long run. Thus randomization ensures a lack of bias, whereas other methods of assignment may not, and the interpretation of an observed group difference in an experiment is largely unambiguous: its cause is the different treatments or conditions received by the two groups. (Many forms of randomization might be employed in designing an experiment, apart from the simple "flipping-a-coin" variety mentioned above; for details see Altman, 1991.)

Randomization alone does not necessarily prevent biased comparisons. Observer judgements may, for example, be affected by knowing the treatment that a subject is getting. This problem is particularly relevant in clinical trials, where it is generally essential to keep both patients and assessors in ignorance of the treatment given, a procedure known as blinding (see Pocock, 1983; for details).

Somewhere between the observational study and the laboratory experiment come studies which attempt to alter the state of affairs in a non-laboratory environment. An example might be, an educational programme designed to prevent smoking, introduced into one school but not another. After a suitable time interval, the programme might be assessed by comparing the two schools on say an outcome measure derived from pupils' responses to a questionnaire that asks how often they smoke. This is not a rigorous experiment since it leaves many conditions uncontrolled, for example, possible differences between the backgrounds of the children who attend the two schools. Nevertheless, because such investigations are designed to come as close as possible to the ideal of a laboratory experiment they are generally termed quasi-experimental.

## DESIGNS FOR EXPERIMENTS

"There are only a handful of ways to do a study properly but a thousand ways to do it wrong" (Sackett, 1986, p. 1328). The issue of the variability of observations made on human and animal subjects was briefly touched upon above. It is such variability that necessitates a statistical approach both to the design and analysis of data from psychological experiments. Many of the principles of experimental design are aimed at trying to control sources of variation that are not of primary interest, so that attention can be focused on variability that is of concern. Some sources of variability may be known, or suspected, but often much remains unexplained. Altman (1991) gives an example involving variability in birth weight. Several variables are known which affect birth weight, including length of gestation, foetal sex, parity, maternal smoking, height above sea level, and so on, but statistical models incorporating such information explain only about one-quarter of the variability in birth weight. While there are undoubtedly other factors not yet identified that contribute to the variability, it is most unlikely that any important factors remain unidentified. The bulk of the observed variability must therefore be considered unexplanable; it is what is known as random variation. Such variation might be considered "background noise" against which it is hoped to detect some effect of interest. The simple, two-group design (see above), for example, attempts to detect a between group difference among the inherent variability of the individual observations. A simple extension of this type of design to more than two groups is one of the simplest experimental procedures used by psychologists. It may be used to illustrate many points concerning the design and subsequent analysis of experiments.

## One-way designs

Suppose an investigator is interested in evaluating the effectiveness of three methods of teaching a given course. Thirty subjects are available who are considered to be a representative sample from the population of interest (important when drawing inferences about the population from the results found in the sample). Three subgroups of ten subjects each are formed at random, and each subgroup taught by one of the three methods. Upon completion of the course, each subject is given the same test covering the material in the course. A possible set of test scores are given in Table 2. How can these scores be used to shed light on whether or not the three teaching methods are equally effective?

The answer involves the comparison of two variances, one of which measures variation between the observations within the three groups, the

*Table 2*   Teaching methods data

| Method 1 | Method 2 | Method 3 |
|----------|----------|----------|
| 10 | 8 | 7 |
| 12 | 9 | 6 |
| 11 | 10 | 5 |
| 8 | 12 | 9 |
| 13 | 11 | 10 |
| 7 | 8 | 9 |
| 14 | 12 | 10 |
| 11 | 11 | 10 |
| 6 | 7 | 10 |
| 12 | 8 | 7 |

23

other of which assesses the variation between the group means. It can be shown that, if the teaching methods are equally effective, then both these sample variances estimate the same population value, so should, within the limits of random sampling, be equal. A statistical test ($F$ test) is available which allows the investigator to judge whether or not it is reasonable to assume that the two variances, are estimates of the same population value and hence to conclude whether or not the teaching methods are equally effective. The procedure is a simple example of a technique known as analysis of variance, introduced by Ronald A. Fisher in the 1920s. Table 3 sets out the relevant results for the data in Table 2. The various terms in Table 3, for example, DF (degrees of freedom), MS (mean square), and so on, are explained in more detail in Weiner (1971).

Essentially what the analysis reported in Table 3 has achieved is a partition of the total variation in the observations into two parts: the first, due to differences between the mean scores for the three teaching methods and the second, due to random variation. If the former is "large" compared to the latter, a group difference is claimed (where "large" is assessed formally by means of the $F$ test). The results here suggest that there is no difference between the teaching methods, since the relevant $F$ statistic is not significant.

The validity of the $F$ test used here is based on certain assumptions which should be briefly mentioned. The first is that the test scores follow a normal distribution and the second is that the variation of these test scores is the same for each of the teaching methods – the homogeneity of variance assumption. If these assumptions are not met then the $F$ test is not strictly correct. There is considerable evidence however, that the test is robust to moderate departures from both assumptions.

If the hypothesis that the teaching methods are equally effective had been rejected, it would not necessarily imply that they all differ, and further analyses may be required to examine the differences in more detail. Such analyses often involve multiple comparison tests described in Bruning and Kintz

Table 3 Analysis of variance table for teaching methods data in Table 2

| Source | SS | DF | MS | F | p |
|--------|------|-----|-------|------|------|
| Method | 22.47 | 2 | 11.23 | 2.43 | 0.11 |
| Error | 124.90 | 27 | 4.62 | | |

Notes:
SS = sum of squares (the sum of the squared deviations of scores from their means)
DF = degrees of freedom (the number of squared deviations minus one)
MS = mean square (the sum of squares divided by the corresponding degrees of freedom)
F = the ratio of the mean square associated with the method divided by the mean square associated with the error
p = the probability of an F ratio at least as large occurring by chance alone, if the methods are equally effective

(1977, pt 3) Weiner (1971, chap. 3), and in detail by Hochberg and Tamhane (1987).

## Factorial designs

Experiments in psychology frequently involve more than a single grouping variable. In the teaching methods example, for instance, it may be thought that age has some effect, and the experimenter may wish to consider separately subjects in the age ranges 10–12 years, 13–15 years, and 16–18 years. The two experimental factors, teaching method and age group, could be considered independently of each other using the procedure outlined above. This would, however, shed no light on their combined effect, which may not be simply the sum of their separate effects. In such cases a factorial design can be used to evaluate possible interaction effects between the grouping factors.

Suppose, for example, fifteen children from each age group are available, five might be randomly assigned to each teaching method and then test scores

Table 4   Teaching methods and age group data

|             | Method 1 | Method 2 | Method 3 |
|-------------|----------|----------|----------|
| 10–12 years | 10       | 8        | 9        |
|             | 8        | 7        | 10       |
|             | 9        | 7        | 12       |
|             | 8        | 9        | 14       |
|             | 10       | 10       | 12       |
| 13–15 years | 11       | 9        | 8        |
|             | 10       | 8        | 9        |
|             | 10       | 8        | 11       |
|             | 15       | 10       | 12       |
|             | 9        | 11       | 11       |
| 16–18 years | 13       | 8        | 7        |
|             | 12       | 7        | 8        |
|             | 14       | 6        | 5        |
|             | 10       | 9        | 7        |
|             | 15       | 10       | 8        |

*Analysis of variance table*

| Source       | SS    | DF | MS    | F    | p        |
|--------------|-------|----|-------|------|----------|
| Age          | 5.91  | 2  | 2.95  | 1.10 | 0.34     |
| Method       | 45.91 | 2  | 22.95 | 8.57 | < 0.001  |
| Age × method | 86.09 | 4  | 21.52 | 8.04 | < 0.001  |
| Error        | 96.40 | 36 | 2.68  |      |          |

*Note*: For abbreviations see Table 3

recorded as in the previous example. A possible set of results is shown in Table 4. Again using the analysis of variance procedure the total variation in the observations can be separated into components representing variation between age group means, variation between teaching method means, variation due to the age group/teaching method interaction, and random error variation. Each of these may be used in an $F$ test to assess whether the data suggest equivalent population effects. Here the analysis of variance indicates the presence of a statistically significant interaction effect, and it is important to consider exactly what this implies.

The simplest method for interpreting an interaction effect is by plotting a graph of appropriate mean values. The relevant plot for the teaching styles/age group example is shown in Figure 1. Examining this plot it can be seen that, for the younger age group, teaching method 3 produces the best results, but for the oldest age group, it leads to the lowest mean value. Because of the presence of this significant interaction, the significant main effect of method seen in the analysis of variance table is largely ignored. The

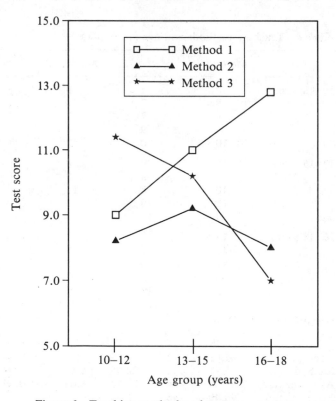

*Figure 1*   Teaching method and age group means

finding of most consequence is that which teaching method is best depends on the age group of the children being taught.

Factorial designs are not restricted to two grouping variables. In the teaching styles, study for example, the investigator may have some a priori evidence (from previous work, etc.) that the sex of a student may need to be

*Table 5*  Teaching method, age group, and sex data

|  |  | Method 1 | Method 2 | Method 3 |
|---|---|---|---|---|
| Male | 10–12 years | 10 | 6 | 8 |
|  |  | 8 | 7 | 12 |
|  |  | 6 | 8 | 13 |
|  |  | 9 | 9 | 14 |
|  | 13–15 years | 6 | 8 | 7 |
|  |  | 8 | 7 | 9 |
|  |  | 9 | 8 | 12 |
|  |  | 8 | 10 | 12 |
|  | 16–18 years | 7 | 12 | 11 |
|  |  | 6 | 12 | 10 |
|  |  | 8 | 10 | 9 |
|  |  | 7 | 9 | 9 |
| Female | 10–12 years | 11 | 8 | 9 |
|  |  | 9 | 9 | 8 |
|  |  | 8 | 7 | 8 |
|  |  | 12 | 12 | 10 |
|  | 13–15 years | 6 | 9 | 12 |
|  |  | 8 | 12 | 11 |
|  |  | 7 | 13 | 9 |
|  |  | 10 | 12 | 12 |
|  | 16–18 years | 12 | 12 | 14 |
|  |  | 8 | 7 | 12 |
|  |  | 7 | 14 | 6 |
|  |  | 13 | 11 | 10 |

*Analysis of variance table*

| Source | SS | DF | MS | F | p |
|---|---|---|---|---|---|
| Age | 5.02 | 2 | 2.51 | 0.64 | 0.53 |
| Method | 41.69 | 2 | 20.85 | 5.34 | 0.01 |
| Sex | 16.05 | 1 | 16.05 | 4.11 | 0.05 |
| Age × method | 31.22 | 4 | 7.80 | 2.00 | 0.11 |
| Age × sex | 6.69 | 2 | 3.35 | 0.86 | 0.43 |
| Method × sex | 16.69 | 2 | 8.35 | 2.14 | 0.13 |
| Age × method × sex | 31.55 | 4 | 7.89 | 2.02 | 0.10 |
| Error | 211.00 | 54 | 3.91 |  |  |

*Note*: For abbreviations see Table 3

considered. Consequently, sex could be added to give a three-way factorial design. A possible data set and corresponding analysis of variance table is shown in Table 5. Here the division of the total variation in the observations is into quite a large number of components corresponding to what are usually termed main effects (age, method, and sex), first-order interactions (age × method, age × sex, and method × sex), and second-order interactions (age × sex × method). Several graphs might be needed in the interpretation of significant interaction effects.

Clearly factorial designs become increasingly complex as the number of factors is increased. A further problem is that the number of subjects required for a complete factorial design quickly become prohibitively large so that alternative designs need to be considered which are more economical in terms of subjects. Perhaps the most common of these is the latin-square (described in detail in Winer, 1971, chap. 10). Here economy in number of subjects required is achieved by assuming a priori that there are no interactions between the factors.

### Within-subject repeated-measure designs

In the discussion of the differences between experimental and observational studies, the advantages of random allocation in the former were described: foremost among these was the balance achieved in the groups on differences between subjects existing prior to the experiment. An alternative approach to eliminating individual differences is to use the same subjects for all conditions. Such studies are known as within-subjects or repeated-measure designs. In such designs any individual peculiarities are equalized out over all conditions.

To illustrate this type of design consider a study in which ten phobic patients are each given three possible treatments and their level of anxiety then recorded. A possible set of data is shown in Table 6.

The analysis of such designs poses more problems than these considered earlier since, to the extent that characteristics of individual subjects remain constant in the different conditions, pairs of observations on the same subject will tend to be correlated rather than independent as assumed previously. Unless these correlations conform to a particular pattern, the usual $F$ tests are no longer applicable. Alternative tests and analysis procedures are described in Greenhouse and Geisser (1959), Hand and Taylor (1987), and Huynh and Feldt (1970).

In the example shown in Table 6, a number of other features of good design need comment. It would, for example, not be sensible to administer the treatments in the same order to each subject, since then the effect of occasion would be confounded with the treatment effect. The order in which a subject is administered the treatments is instead randomized. It would also be important to allow sufficient time between the administration of each

*Table 6*  Simple example of a repeated-measures design

| Subject | Treatment 1 | Treatment 2 | Treatment 3 |
|---------|-------------|-------------|-------------|
| 1  | 3 | 5 | 5 |
| 2  | 4 | 7 | 6 |
| 3  | 2 | 3 | 3 |
| 4  | 5 | 4 | 6 |
| 5  | 3 | 6 | 7 |
| 6  | 2 | 4 | 5 |
| 7  | 2 | 3 | 5 |
| 8  | 6 | 7 | 9 |
| 9  | 3 | 6 | 7 |
| 10 | 4 | 4 | 5 |

treatment to avoid the possible effects of one treatment on the effect of subsequent treatments.

Such possible carry-over effects are particular important in the commonly used $2 \times 2$ crossover design, in which two treatments are to be compared. Here subjects are randomly allocated to one of two groups: in one group the subjects receive treatment $A$ followed by treatment $B$, in the other group subjects receive the treatments in the reverse order. Note that this design has both a between-subjects component, the different orders of administration of the two treatments, and a within-subjects component, the measurements made on each subject for both treatments. An example of the practical application of such a design is provided by Broota (1989), where an experimenter is interested in testing the effect of caffeine on a tracking task. Two doses of caffeine are used (5 mg and 10 mg), each subject being observed under each dose, and scored on a measure of dexterity. The experiment was conducted at two different periods of the day (morning and evening) five subjects being randomly assigned to the order 5 mg, 10 mg, and a further five to 10 mg, 5 mg. The data are shown in Table 7.

There are several difficult issues involved in the analysis of what appears to be a relatively simple design. They are discussed in detail in Armitage and Hills (1982), Brown (1980), and Jones and Kenward (1989). Major problems are the detection of possible carry-over effects and their impact on the assessment of the treatment effect. In general the design can be used with confidence only when a carry-over effect can be discounted a priori. In the caffeine experiment, for example, the interval between the two tests was considered large enough to dissipate the effect of the earlier dose. The appropriate analysis of variance table for the data in Table 7 is shown in Table 8. Here the test for group differences in the between subjects section is equivalent to testing for a carry-over effect. The result confirms that for these data there is no such effect. In the within-subjects section it is seen that the occasion effect is non-significant and the group $\times$ occasion interaction is highly

*Table 7*  2 × 2 crossover study: two doses of caffeine

|  | Subject | Morning | Evening |
|---|---|---|---|
| Group 1 (5 mg, 10 mg) | 1 | 15 | 24 |
|  | 2 | 16 | 25 |
|  | 3 | 17 | 24 |
|  | 4 | 14 | 22 |
|  | 5 | 16 | 22 |
| Group 2 (10 mg, 5 mg) | 6 | 22 | 18 |
|  | 7 | 23 | 15 |
|  | 8 | 21 | 17 |
|  | 9 | 22 | 18 |
|  | 10 | 25 | 17 |

*Table 8*  Analysis of variance for crossover data

| Analysis of variance table | | | | | |
|---|---|---|---|---|---|
| Source | SS | DF | MS | F | p |
| Between subjects | | | | | |
| Group | 0.45 | 1 | 0.45 | 0.23 | 0.63 |
| Error | 14.60 | 8 | 1.83 | | |
| Within subjects | | | | | |
| Occasion | 6.05 | 1 | 6.05 | 3.71 | 0.09 |
| Group × occasion (caffeine) | 224.45 | 1 | 224.45 | 137.70 | < 0.0001 |
| Error | 13.00 | 8 | 1.63 | | |

*Note*: For abbreviations see Table 3

significant. With this type of design the test for this interaction corresponds to a test of the treatment main effect, in this case a test of the difference in the two doses of caffeine. Here the higher dose of caffeine clearly produces higher dexterity scores on the tracking task.

## ANALYSIS OF COVARIANCE

In the 1930s Fisher introduced the technique known as the analysis of covariance as a means of reducing error variation and increasing the sensitivity of an analysis of variance for detecting mean differences. The method depends upon identifying one or more measurements known as covariates, which are related to the response variable but not to the experimental treatment condition. (This is most often assured by measuring the covariate prior to the administration of the treatment.) By including such concomitant measures in the analysis, residual variation can be reduced by the extent to which it is attributable to the covariates. As an example, consider again the teaching methods experiment. Here a useful covariate might be a test score for each subject recorded before the experiment began. (Such a data set is given in Table 9.) A possible method for introducing this covariate into the analysis of the data would be to simply subtract it from the test score observed at the completion of the experiment. The one-way analysis of variance would then be applied to the difference scores (see Table 10). A more formal procedure is to assume that the dependent variable is related to the covariate in some way and use this assumed relationship for the purpose of adjustment. Details of such models are given in Winer (1971). An appropriate analysis for the data in Table 9 is shown in Table 11. The analyses in Tables 10 and 11 do not change the original conclusion that the teaching methods do not differ. In each case, however, the error mean square is much lower than in the simple analysis of variance shown in Table 3. Note also that the error term in the analysis of covariance has lost a degree of freedom due to the estimation of the relationship between final and initial scores.

When the analysis of variance procedure is used in experiments involving random allocation of subjects to groups it is generally a completely acceptable approach to deriving more sensitive tests. Unfortunately it is often used by psychologists in the hope of overcoming the disadvantages of studies

*Table 9*  Teaching methods data-initial and final scores

| Method 1 | | Method 2 | | Method 3 | |
|---------|-------|---------|-------|---------|-------|
| *Initial* | *Final* | *Initial* | *Final* | *Initial* | *Final* |
| 7 | 10 | 6 | 8 | 4 | 7 |
| 9 | 12 | 5 | 9 | 5 | 6 |
| 9 | 11 | 7 | 10 | 5 | 5 |
| 8 | 8 | 11 | 12 | 6 | 9 |
| 12 | 13 | 10 | 11 | 6 | 10 |
| 8 | 7 | 6 | 8 | 7 | 9 |
| 11 | 14 | 12 | 12 | 9 | 10 |
| 10 | 11 | 9 | 11 | 10 | 10 |
| 3 | 6 | 5 | 7 | 9 | 10 |
| 8 | 12 | 7 | 8 | 7 | 7 |

*Table 10*  Analysis of variance for differences between final and initial scores in Table 9

| Source | SS | DF | MS | F | p |
|--------|------|----|------|------|------|
| Methods | 0.87 | 2 | 0.43 | 0.22 | 0.80 |
| Error | 53.00 | 27 | 1.96 | | |

*Note*: For abbreviations see Table 3

Table 11  Analysis of covariance for teaching methods data-initial score used as covariate

| Source | SS | DF | MS | F | p |
|--------|------|----|------|------|------|
| Method | 3.30 | 2 | 1.65 | 0.99 | 0.38 |
| Error | 43.27 | 26 | 1.66 | | |

*Note*: For abbreviations see Table 3

where randomization is not possible. An investigator may, for example, be interested in determining whether normal subjects have different reaction times from those diagnosed as schizophrenic and those diagnosed as depressed. A variable which clearly affects reaction time is age, and this may be introduced as a covariate, and analysis of covariance used to adjust the comparisons of reaction time across the three groups for the possibly different group age distributions.

Although such an approach may be helpful in particular instances there are possible problems. First, there may be variables other than the observed covariate, age, that affect reaction time. Unless age acts as a surrogate for all of these the comparison between groups could still be misleading. Second, after performing the analysis of covariance the investigator will have an answer to the question, "Conditional on having the same age, does the reaction time of normals, schizophrenics, and depressives differ?" In some circumstances, however, this might not be a sensible question: suppose, for example, that patients diagnosed as schizophrenic were always younger than those with the diagnosis, depression? Such difficulties are discussed in detail in Fleiss and Tanur (1972).

## CONCLUSION

The good design of experiments in psychology is essential if valid conclusions are to be drawn. One of the corner-stones of a well-designed experiment is randomization, a procedure which can only partially be replaced by methods such as analysis of covariance which purport to offer some form of statistical control. In situations where randomization is not an option, the quasi-experimental approach might be used. A feature of designing experiments not mentioned in this chapter is that concerning the number of subjects needed in a study; this important problem is dealt with in detail by Pocock (1983).

Psychologists need to be familiar with the basics of experimental design and with methods of analysis such as analysis of variance. Nowadays, of course, they need not be familiar with the arithmetic of such procedures, since the ubiquitous personal computer can perform even the most complex analyses in a few seconds. This is not, however, without potential dangers and experimental psychologists need to ensure that they are familiar with exactly what type of analysis has been performed. A visit to a statistician may often be necessary!

## FURTHER READING

Campbell, D. T., & Stanley, J. C. (1963). *Experimental and quasi-experimental designs for research*. Chicago, IL: Rand McNally.
Cox, D. R. (1958). *Planning of experiments*. New York: Wiley.
Mead, R. (1989). *The design of experiments*. Cambridge: Cambridge University Press.
Myers, A. (1980). *Experimental psychology*. New York: Van Norstrand.

## REFERENCES

Altman, D. G. (1991). *Practical statistics for medical research*. London: Chapman & Hall.
Armitage, P., & Hills, M. (1982). The two-period crossover trial. *The Statistician, 31*, 119–131.
Broota, K. D. (1989). *Experimental design in behavioural research*. New Delhi: Wiley.
Brown, B. W. (1980). The crossover experiment for clinical trials. *Biometrics, 36*, 69–79.
Bruning, J. L., & Kintz, R. L. (1977). *Comparative handbook of statistics* (2nd edn). Glenview, IL: Scott, Foresman.
Dunn, G. (1989). *Design and analysis of reliability studies*. Sevenoaks: Edward Arnold.
Everitt, B. S. (1989). *Statistical methods for medical investigations*. Sevenoaks: Edward Arnold.
Fleiss, J. L. (1986). *The design and analysis of clinical experiments*. New York: Wiley.
Fleiss, J. L., & Tanur, J. M. (1972). The analysis of covariance in psychopathology. In M. Hammer, K. Salzinger, & S. Sutton (Eds) *Psychopathology: Contributions from the social, behavioural and biological sciences* (pp. 509–527). New York: Wiley.
Greenhouse, S. W., & Geisser, S. (1959). On the methods in the analysis of profile data. *Psychometrika, 24*, 95–112.
Hand, D. J. & Taylor, C. C. (1987). *Multivariate analysis of variance and repeated measures*. London: Chapman & Hall.
Hochberg, Y., & Tamhane, A. C. (1987). *Multiple comparison procedures*. New York: Wiley.
Huynh, H., & Feldt, L. S. (1970). Conditions under which mean square ratios in repeated measurement designs have exact $F$ distributions. *Journal of the American Statistical Association, 65*, 1582–1589.
Jones, B., & Kenward, M. G. (1989). *Design and analysis of cross-over trials*. London: Chapman & Hall.
Pocock, S. J. (1983). *Clinical trials*. Chichester: Wiley.
Sackett, D. L. (1986). Rational therapy in the neurosciences: The role of the randomized trial. *Stroke, 17*, 1323–1329.

Schontz, F. C. (1986). *Funadmentals of research in the behavioral Sciences.* Washington, DC: American Psychiatric Press.

Winer, B. J. (1971). *Statistical principles in experimental design.* New York: McGraw-Hill.

# 3

# DESCRIPTIVE AND INFERENTIAL STATISTICS

## A. W. MacRae

### University of Birmingham, England

| | |
|---|---|
| **Descriptive statistics** | Frequencies |
| Types of data | Univariate measures |
| Scales of measurement | Bivariate measures |
| Graphical descriptions | Multivariate measures |
| Numerical summaries | Nonparametric statistics |
| **Inferential statistics** | Directional and non- |
| The logic of classical | directional tests |
| statistical inference | Multiple comparisons: |
| Bayesian inference | planned and unplanned |
| Bayesian or classical | **Parameter estimation and** |
| methods? | **confidence intervals** |
| Inferential statistics for | **Further reading** |
| different types of data | **References** |

When we have a body of data – numbers that describe some aspect of the world that interests us – and hope to learn something useful from it, two approaches are available: descriptive and inferential statistics. For example, if we have information about 100 children we may want to say things about the particular individuals studied, so we quantify their abilities, classify their social interactions, and so on. These are descriptions (using descriptive statistics) which summarize the data we actually obtained; that may be useful when advising these children or their parents but does not tell us anything about other children. Alternatively, we might perform an experiment to evaluate a teaching method. We then want the data to tell us something about the response of children in general. Because we cannot try out the method with all children we must do so with a sample of children – perhaps 100 again. Our analysis now uses the information from the sample to make inferences (using inferential statistics) about what to expect from the much larger group of children we have not studied. A wider group to which we hope to generalize our results is called a population.

## DESCRIPTIVE STATISTICS

Even small collections of data can be hard to understand until they are simplified by organizing the original numbers to make their overall pattern clearer or summarizing them by calculating a few numbers that capture as much as possible of the original information.

A stem-and-leaf diagram organizes a collection of numbers with no loss of information. The two sets of numbers in Table 1 contain exactly the same information, but in the stem-and-leaf diagram (1b) the first two digits of the number are represented by a row in the table. For example, the number 137 contributes to the row labelled "13". The third digit of each number is written in the appropriate row. For example, the top row of 1b represents the numbers 105, 107, 107, 108, and 109. When organized in that way, it becomes obvious that numbers between 155 and 170 did not occur, whereas that fact (which might be quite important when dealing with real measurements) is not at all obvious in the unorganized list of numbers in 1a.

*Table 1* Organizing data without losing any information can reveal attributes originally hidden

| *1a Raw data as originally obtained* | | | | | *1b The same data organized in a stem-and-leaf diagram* |
|---|---|---|---|---|---|
| 137 | 111 | 134 | 147 | 110 | |
| 185 | 173 | 183 | 115 | 185 | 10 57789 |
| 114 | 113 | 137 | 187 | 126 | 11 00011233455568 |
| 110 | 112 | 121 | 175 | 171 | 12 0011345679 |
| 147 | 192 | 110 | 179 | 125 | 13 3347788 |
| 183 | 190 | 116 | 191 | 115 | 14 47799 |
| 177 | 185 | 183 | 154 | 107 | 15 1444 |
| 149 | 109 | 184 | 191 | 149 | 16 |
| 138 | 120 | 178 | 154 | 173 | 17 11233356789 |
| 144 | 176 | 184 | 113 | 120 | 18 00222333444555578 |
| 182 | 182 | 184 | 188 | 151 | 19 0111223 |
| 171 | 154 | 129 | 115 | 121 | |
| 185 | 105 | 182 | 107 | 138 | |
| 180 | 118 | 108 | 191 | 172 | |
| 173 | 123 | 124 | 133 | 193 | |
| 111 | 127 | 192 | 133 | 180 | |

A box-and-whisker plot is a pictorial summary of data, where the "box" indicates the range of scores that omits the highest 25 per cent and lowest 25 per cent of all scores, the mid-line indicates the median (the score exceeded by exactly 50 per cent of all the scores) while the whiskers indicate the extreme range of high and low scores. Unlike the stem-and-leaf diagram, a box-and-whisker plot is just a summary which does not allow us to identify all the original numbers because it captures only some of their attributes. However, what it captures may be all we need, and because it is a very simplified representation of the original table it may be good for comparing several sets of data. Figure 1 shows box-and-whisker plots of the data in Table 1. Each column is shown by a different plot – which would be appropriate if each was obtained from a different condition in an experiment, say. They allow us to see that all the columns have much the same range of scores (roughly 105 to 190) but column 2 is noticeably different from the others in having a very low median. That is, half the scores in column 2 lie below 125 whereas only about a quarter of those in columns 1, 3, 4, and 5 do. The strange distribution of values in Table 1 is hinted at by the two halves of the "box" being longer than the two "whiskers" in every case, whereas in a distribution having a peak near the centre, the whiskers would be longer than the box. Other differences between columns can also be seen.

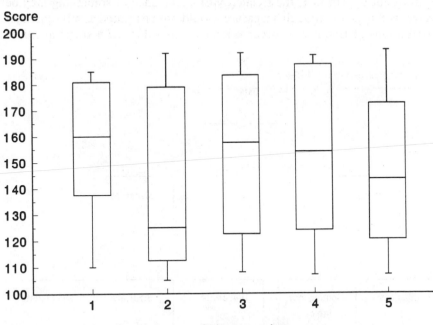

*Figure 1* Box-and-whisker plots, one from each column of the data in Table 1

Techniques for organizing and summarizing data have been described by Tukey (1977), under the name of "Exploratory Data Analysis" (EDA). They are often the best way to start because representing the same data in various ways often lets us see "what is really happening".

## Types of data

We use data to represent aspects of the world by symbols that we can manipulate, tabulate, and so on. (The "aspects of the world" that interest psychologists may be attributes of individuals that are not directly observable.) Often, numerical data result from measurement, but we must distinguish between the numbers and the things we really want to know about. The numbers may allow us to make inferences and predictions about aspects of the world,but they are of little interest in themselves. Levy (1981) comments that when people have what they think is a "statistical" problem it is usually because of uncertainty about how the numbers relate to the question being investigated.

Figure 2 shows one way of classifying types of data. The first division is into "frequencies" and "measures". Frequencies are counts of the number of cases of a particular kind, and obviously must be whole numbers. Measures are numbers that express the amount of something. They may be whole numbers but need not be. (In fact, the frequency of occurrence of something may be treated as a measure, though a measure should not be treated as a frequency.) Distributions of frequencies occur when various values of a single attribute

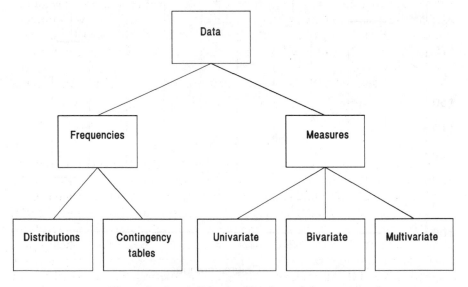

*Figure 2*  A possible classification of data types

are used to divide up the cases into their various categories – for example, if we count the number of children with black, brown, red, or fair hair. Contingency tables (also known as cross-classifications) are generated when two or more attributes are used to divide up the cases – for example, if we classify children as high, medium, and low in anxiety and simultaneously separate them out by hair colour as above, giving twelve categories in all.

Univariate measures vary in only one respect. Examples of univariate data are age, score on a test, family size, and time taken to solve a problem. Multivariate measures vary in several respects. For example, for each individual in our sample we might know the age, the family size, and the score made on a test. That collection of information about the individual is multivariate. Each measure is univariate when considered on its own, but the set of measures is multivariate if we think of them as a composite description of the individual. Of course we can treat such an assembly of measures as multivariate only if they are related together in some way, for example if each measure comes from a single individual. Bivariate data are just a special kind of multivariate data with exactly two measures per individual.

Questionnaires are often best thought of as multivariate measures because each respondent is free to give any pattern of answers and each pattern may have a different meaning. Sometimes all the questions assess the same thing (all are comparable indicators of some political attitude, say) and then you might take no interest in which particular questions received positive answers but count only the number that did. A total score obtained in that way would be univariate. Thus the distinction between these types of data is not clear-cut and is more an expression of opinion about the meaning of the data than a matter of actual fact. However, if we take the view that our data are multivariate, we need different statistical techniques from those used with univariate data. Another source of multivariate information is an experiment where more than one type of result is recorded on each trial – for example, the time taken to respond and also the accuracy of the response made. In some experiments, we may need dozens of separate measures to describe the outcome of each trial and a multivariate analysis should be used.

## Scales of measurement

The classification of data types by Stevens (1946, 1951) describes the relationship between the numbers constituting the data and the "true" value of the thing measured. The numbers are said to conform to a measurement scale which is nominal, ordinal, interval, ratio, or absolute. In a nominal scale, there is no relationship between the size of a number and the value of the thing "measured" by it. A No. 14 bus need not exceed a No. 7 bus in any way – and you would certainly not think of catching two No. 7s if you really wanted a No. 14! All that you can tell from the numbers is whether two things are equivalent in some respect (because they have the same number) or are different (because they have different numbers). In an ordinal scale, the order of sizes of the numbers tells us the order of sizes of the things measured. If item A is assigned a larger number than item B, then A has more of the thing measured. For example, we can often be pretty confident that Arthur is happier than Bernard (though both are quite happy) and Carol is happier than Diana (though both are unhappy). But we probably have no way to decide if the difference in happiness between Arthur and Bernard is greater or smaller than the difference in happiness between Carol and Diana. If we can put such differences in order, we have an ordered metric scale (a fairly common type which is not often mentioned in psychology). If, in addition, we can say when differences are equal we have an interval scale. True interval scales are rather rare because if we can compare differences between pairs of large values and pairs of small values well enough to say if they are equal or not, we usually also know when the thing measured is completely absent, and then we have a ratio scale. In a ratio scale, the number zero denotes absence of the thing measured and equal increases in number denote equal increases in the thing measured. If so, equal ratios between numbers must denote equal ratios in the thing measured, so it makes sense to talk about one measurement being twice as great as another, for example. Most of the familiar measures of daily life, for example weights or distances, are ratio scales, but they are rare for psychological variables. An absolute scale has no freedom to change even the units of measurement and for all practical purposes occurs only when we count things rather than measure them.

In my classification, frequency data correspond to absolute scales while different types of measures correspond to ordinal, interval, ordered metric, or ratio scales. Most numbers used in psychology relate to the relevant aspect of the world by either an absolute scale (counting) or an ordinal scale (measuring). Proving that a psychological measurement is on an interval or ratio scale is more difficult than it is for most physical scales, such as those of length or weight. For the latter, we can easily take a standard unit (a rod 10 mm long, say) and hold it against various sections of a tape measure to show that the difference between 20 and 30 mm is the same as that between 80 and 90 mm. Nothing comparable can be done for measures of most psychological attributes, but for many practical purposes people are willing to assume that measurement is on an interval, or even a ratio, scale and that the difference between levels of ability indicated by scores of 20 and 30 is equivalent to that between scores of 80 and 90 on some well-constructed test.

Some people consider that a scale type being ordinal or interval determines the kinds of statistical treatment that may be appropriate, but I think that view is very often exaggerated (see MacRae, 1988). The distinction between scale types affects the interpretation of numerical results, but is less relevant to the choice of significance test (discussed later). However, the distinction between univariate and multivariate data does affect the type of statistical analysis needed.

## Graphical descriptions

There are many ways to graph one variable against another, each method emphasizing different properties of the relationship and using the power of the human eye and brain to see patterns that might not be detectable in a table of numbers Cleveland (1985) and Tufte (1983) advise on ways to assist the process, with an overview by Cleveland and McGill (1985). Numerical summaries are less trouble to produce, take up less space and can be conveyed orally if necessary, so there is a place for both approaches.

A bar chart shows on one axis the frequency of occurrence of each score (or group of scores) displayed along the other axis. Bar charts can easily be compared if the same units are used in each, and thus can reveal the differences among two or more sets of results. A histogram is a bar chart where the scores have a natural order, that is, they are univariate measures on at least an ordinal scale. A histogram displays the frequency distribution of the measure, from which we can easily see the highest and lowest values that occurred and get a good idea of which scores were frequent and which were rare.

Cross-tabulated frequencies may not be easy to graph. Even if there are only two dimensions of cross-classification, the resulting frequency must be expressed on a third dimension. It is possible to draw a perspective view of a 3D histogram where each slice is a normal histogram or (if the frequencies vary smoothly) it may be useful to draw contour plots, using the conventions of map-making to represent the frequency as though it were a height. Alternatively, the frequency can be expressed as a number of dots, with the two classification dimensions forming the axes of a grid. When there are more than two dimensions of classification it will usually be necessary to draw multiple graphs to represent the data adequately.

Bivariate measures arise when each individual is measured in two different ways. For example, we might give all applicants for a job a test that is designed to predict how well they will perform it, and later assess how well they did in fact perform in their first year. Each individual thus obtains a "Test Score" and later a "Performance Score". The relationship between the two can be expressed in a scatter plot (also called a scattergram) in which each individual appears as a single point. The scales are chosen to give about the same spread on each axis so that the outline of the graph is approximately square.

In each of Figures 3a, 3b, and 3c, we see a tendency for the performance scores to be high if scores on the test were high. In 3a the relationship is very close so it is possible to be fairly confident about the performance to be expected if we know the test score. Figure 3b shows a much weaker relationship. Knowing the test score improves our prediction of performance — our best estimate is higher if the test score high and is lower if the test score is low — but many exceptions occur. In 3c, there is again a strong relationship

41

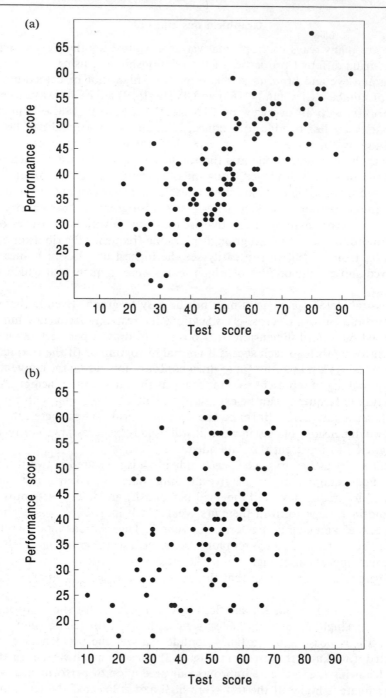

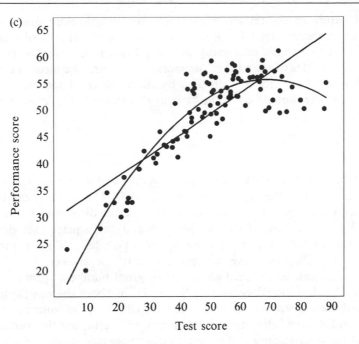

*Figure 3* Scatter plots of imaginary data relating a measure of performance in a job to the score obtained by the same individual in an earlier selection test

but it does not follow a straight line. For test scores above about 40, there is little further increase in the typical performance score. In Figure 3c, the best-fitting straight line and the best-fitting quadratic (curved) line are plotted through the data points and we see that the curved line passes close to more points than does the straight one and so provides a better description of the relationship present in these results.

Multivariate measures can take advantage of our ability to extract patterns visually from complex diagrams if each component is represented by some attribute of a pattern which can then be recognized as a whole. Chernoff (1973) proposed the use of faces, where one component might alter the size of the face, another the curvature of the mouth, another the spacing of the eyes, and so on. There are problems of avoiding undue emphasis on particular components and inappropriate patterns, such as a smiling face to indicate a distressing combination of symptoms, but the approach is interesting. Advice on multivariate graphs can be found in Cleveland (1985), Everitt (1978), and Wainer and Thissen (1981).

### Numerical summaries

Numerical summaries reduce many numbers to just a few which describe the general nature of the results. With frequency distributions and univariate measures, a mean (symbol $\bar{X}$), expressing a typical value, and a standard deviation (symbol SD), expressing the spread of the scores, may be enough to give a good idea of the sorts of numbers that occur. The mean is calculated by adding all the scores and dividing by the number of scores, so it is the measure usually thought of as the "average" value. One formula expressing the SD is

$$SD = \sqrt{\frac{\Sigma(X - \bar{X})^2}{N - 1}}$$

The symbol $\Sigma$ is the Greek capital letter sigma, and is an instruction to add up all the values of the expression that follows it. The formula can be interpreted as a sequence of instructions, thus: find the difference between each score ($X$) and the mean ($\bar{X}$) (that is, its deviation); square each deviation; add up the results; divide the answer by ($N - 1$), where $N$ is the number of scores in the collection; take the square root of the answer.

How much can be deduced about the original numbers from their mean and standard deviation depends on what we know about the way the numbers are distributed. If we have no idea of the distribution, the summary given by a mean and standard deviation may not be very useful, but the median (midpoint of the distribution) and inter-quartile range (the spread of the middle 50 per cent of the scores) give a description that can always be interpreted. (It is these, together with the highest and lowest scores, that are displayed in box-and-whisker plots.)

Descriptive methods for cross-tabulated frequencies usually concern relationships between the categories forming the rows and columns of the table. In the example of hair colour and anxiety proposed earlier, we might be interested in discovering if those with one hair colour are more likely than those with another to be rated high on anxiety. Another example would be where two clinicians make independent assessments of the same clients. We might then be interested in characterizing the extent of their agreement. Various measures can be used for each of these purposes, all with somewhat different meanings (Leach, 1979).

The product-moment correlation ($r$) also known as Pearson correlation, is a measure of how well bivariate data fit a straight-line plot on a scattergram. If the line slopes up, as in Figures 3a, 3b, and 3c, the value of $r$ will be positive. If it slopes down, $r$ will be negative. If there is no trend up or down, $r$ will be zero. There are several ways to calculate $r$, including this one

$$r = \frac{\Sigma(X - \bar{X})(Y - \bar{Y})}{\sqrt{\Sigma(X - \bar{X})^2 \Sigma(Y - \bar{Y})^2}}$$

In this formula, $X$ represents scores on one of the variables and $Y$ represents corresponding scores on the other.

The value of $r$ does not measure any other kind of relationship than a straight line, so it should not be interpreted as measuring relatedness in general. We must not interpret a small or zero correlation as showing that there is little relationship between the variables — it may be close but not linear, as in Figure 3c.

If we believe that product-moment correlation underestimates relatedness because the variables are related in a non-linear way, we may use a variant called multiple correlation (or multiple regression) to express curvilinear relatedness. It can also be used to express the way that a single variable is related to several others. For example, success in a course might be separately predictable from intelligence, time spent studying, ambition to succeed, and previous knowledge of the subject. Knowing an individual's score on all four of these predictors would surely permit better prediction than any one of them on its own, and the multiple correlation of all the predictors with success would express the closeness of the agreement between prediction and outcome.

## INFERENTIAL STATISTICS

There are several styles of statistical inference, but the dominant one, referred to as "classical" statistics, draws conclusions about "statistical significance". These inferences invoke the notion of probability. That is, we do not conclude that something is true or false but that there is some chance of it being true or false, which can be described by a number between 0 and 1, where 0 indicates that there is no chance and 1 indicates certainty. The chance that a fair coin will fall heads when tossed is .5 because there are two possible outcomes and both are equally likely.

The methods of classical statistics evaluate the possibility that when a result looks interesting, it is merely the uninteresting variability in the measurements that has caused it. To eliminate that disappointing explanation, significance tests calculate the probability of obtaining results like those actually obtained if chance alone is the true explanation. If the probability is small, then the explanation that chance alone is responsible seems less reasonable. If it is small enough, the result is said to be statistically significant. By convention, results are usually considered significant if the probability is no larger than .05 (1 in 20), and for some purposes other levels such as .01 and .001 may be quoted. Note however that showing a result to be significant only disposes of chance as an acceptable explanation for result: a significance test does not endorse any other explanation in particular. It is the task of experimental design to ensure that just one satisfactory explanation is left after chance is eliminated.

### The logic of classical statistical inference

Consider the following (non-statistical) hypotheses, $H_a$ and $H_b$, that you

45

might be entertaining about my possible location at this moment and two alternative items of information I might give you (possible observations, $O_c$ and $O_d$) to help you to decide where I am:

$H_a$: I am at the top of a mountain in Wales
$H_b$: I am *not* at the top of a mountain in Wales
$O_c$: I can see a double-decker bus within ten yards of me
$O_d$: I can *not* see a double-decker bus within ten yards of me.

One or other of the hypotheses must be true, and also one or other of the observations must occur. Now consider what each of the possible observations tells you about the truth of each of the hypotheses. If I give you information $O_c$, you should feel very inclined to reject hypothesis $H_a$ – you probably think it most unlikely that I should see a double-decker bus at the top of a mountain. If so, you will be pretty confident that $H_b$ is true, so in this case you make a decision in favour of one hypothesis out of two that between them cover all the possibilities.

However, if the information I give you is $O_d$, reporting that I can *not* see a double-decker bus, you are certainly not obliged to conclude that I am on a Welsh mountain! This time, the information does not induce you to reject one hypothesis and accept the other. Thus there may be a lack of symmetry about the sorts of inference that observations allow us to make about hypotheses. The difference between $H_a$ and $H_b$ is that the first is very specific and the second is very general: it excludes absolutely nothing except the one possibility mentioned by $H_a$. The null hypothesis invoked in classical statistics is also very specific: it declares that the true difference between groups is exactly zero. The alternative hypothesis includes absolutely every other possibility, including the possibility that there is some real but very tiny difference. For that reason, there is a lack of symmetry about the inferences to be made about the null hypothesis too.

The probability given by a test of significance is thus the probability of obtaining such results if the null hypothesis is exactly true and chance is the only explanation for the observations. But that is not the probability that chance is the only explanation. To clarify that point, consider the following probabilities:

(a) Probability that (I visit Westminster Abbey) if (I am in London) = .01
(b) Probability that (I am in London) if (I visit Westminster Abbey) = 1.00

For everyone, (b), the probability of being in London when visiting Westminster Abbey, is 1.00. The probability (a) of visiting Westminster Abbey when in London will be different for each person, and will hardly ever be 1.00.

Therefore, the probabilities described by (a) and (b) are different, even though the phrases look rather similar. Now consider the following:

(c) Probability that (I get such results) if (the null hypothesis is true) = .05
(d) Probability that (the null hypothesis is true) if (I get such results) = ?

The probabilities (a) and (b) are different, but the relationship between (a) and (b) is exactly the same as that between (c) and (d), so the probabilities described by (c) and (d) are different also. A test of significance gives us a value for (c) but does not tell us the value of (d), so we do not know how likely it is that the null hypothesis is true.

Now suppose our result is non-significant, that is, the probability of obtaining results like ours is *greater* than .05. Even if we find that the probability of obtaining such results when chance is the only cause is very high, say .9, *we should not conclude that chance is likely to be the only cause.* The significance test shows that chance *can* easily explain the results but it does not estimate the probability that it *did* give us the results. In fact, a conventional test of significance lets us conclude nothing useful if the result is not significant.

If the aim of our study is to show that two treatments differ, then a significant result is helpful, because it makes mere chance unattractive as an explanation. (Telling you that I can see a bus makes a Welsh mountaintop an unlikely location.) If our aim is to show that they are *not* different, a non-significant result is of no real help. (Telling you that I can not see a bus gives you hardly any information about my location since it can be true practically anywhere.) That limitation on the inferences to be drawn from significance tests is a serious one, and too little attention is paid in psychology to the main ways of dealing with the problem: classical confidence intervals (discussed later) and Bayesian inference.

### Bayesian inference

Bayesian methods address the question we really want to answer when faced with data that may support an interesting conclusion: "How likely is it that the interesting conclusion is correct?" Compared with the huge number of books and papers about classical methods, there are few about Bayesian methods and only one textbook for psychologists (Phillips, 1973).

Bayesian methods evaluate the probabilities of observing the data, $D$, if Hypothesis $A$ is correct, written $p(D|H_A)$, and if possibility $B$ is correct, written $p(D|H_B)$. These correspond to the calculations in classical inference of the probability of obtaining the data given that the null hypothesis, $H_O$, is correct. But Bayesian methods invoke an additional relationship named

"Bayes Rule" after the eighteenth-century Revd Thomas Bayes, who wrote about it:

$$p(H_A|D) = p(H_A) \frac{p(D|H_A)}{p(D)}$$

It signifies that the probability of Hypothesis $A$ being true, given the observed data, is found by multiplying the probability of Hypothesis $A$ being true anyway, $p(H_A)$, by the probability of obtaining the data if Hypothesis $A$ is true, $p(D|H_A)$, and dividing the answer by the probability of obtaining the data without stating what hypothesis is true, $p(D)$.

In that form, the result is not very useful, since the probability of obtaining the data can be calculated only when we have adopted a particular hypothesis. However, if the analogous expression is calculated for the probability of Hypothesis $B$ being true, and the first expression is divided by the second, we obtain the more useful result where the unknown probability, $p(D)$, is cancelled out:

$$\frac{p(H_A|D)}{p(H_B|D)} = \frac{p(H_A)}{p(H_B)} \frac{p(D|H_A)}{p(D|H_B)}$$

On the left of the equation, the relative probabilities of Hypotheses $A$ and $B$ being correct in the light of the data is calculated from (on the right of the equation) their relative probabilities before obtaining the data and the relative probabilities of the data under Hypotheses $A$ and $B$ respectively. The calculations and data thus alter our previous opinion about the relative probabilities of hypotheses $A$ and $B$. If we are at first strongly convinced that $A$ is correct, we need strong evidence to persuade us that $B$ is the correct explanation and the evidence consists of the relative probabilities of obtaining these results when $A$ is true and when $B$ is true. The data need not be *likely* if $B$ is the true explanation – only much *less* likely if $A$ is true.

Considering in this way the hypotheses about my location, the information that I can see a bus is not particularly likely at any time. We can write that as $p(O_c|H_b) = .001$, say, to indicate that the probability, that I can see a bus, $O_c$, is one in a thousand even on the hypothesis, $H_b$, that I am not on a mountain. But the probability of seeing a bus, $O_c$, is very much smaller if I *am* on a mountain, $H_a$ – surely not more than 1 in 1 million, so $p(O_c|H_a) = .000001$. The ratio of $p(O_c|H_b)$ to $p(O_c|H_a)$ is thus at least 1,000 to 1, so whatever prior ratio of probabilities you had for me being on a mountain as opposed to not being on a mountain, it is decreased by a factor of at least 1,000 after you are told that I can see a bus.

Had the data indicated that I can *not* see a bus, $O_d$, the information has little effect. That result has very high likelihood (.99999) if I am on a mountain, but is almost as high (.99000) if I am not on a mountain, so it causes hardly any increase (the ratio is only 1.01 to 1) in what was originally a very small likelihood of being on a Welsh mountaintop.

## Bayesian or classical methods?

Some people dislike the Bayesian style of argument because it explicitly refers to our prior beliefs about the relative likelihoods of the theories under test, but that is a mistaken objection. Classical methods focus on a precise null hypothesis and see if the results have a probability under it that is small enough to be significant. That appears not to invoke prior beliefs, but if we ask what counts as "significant" we find that it depends on the plausibility of the alternative hypotheses available. For example, we may be convinced that one training method is better than another if a result is significant at the .05 level, but if an experiment is so well done that chance is the only alternative, many people would still prefer to believe in chance than accept .05 significance as proof of extrasensory perception. Similarly, people usually consider a result that is significant at the .01 level more convincing than one significant at the .05 level. That way of thinking is quite contrary to the logical structure of classical statistics because the latter views a set of results as falling into one or other of two categories of outcome: a rejection region, and a non-rejection region. The range of possible outcomes constituting the rejection region is decided in advance and the probability of falling in it by chance alone – of falling anywhere in it – is the significance level of the result. That is the formal structure, but, (as noted above) most of those who use it do not follow it in detail. Rather, they reach conclusions in a way that is approximately Bayesian.

There have been interesting developments in France using Bayesian logic. Most of the publications are in French, but there are some in English (e.g., Rouanet & Lecoutre, 1983; Rouanet, Lépine, & Pelnard-Considère, 1976). The approach may allow psychologists to address directly the questions they usually want to ask, that is, to decide how likely a particular conclusion is in the light of the data rather than following the back-to-front classical approach of testing a null hypothesis they do not believe in the first place with a view to rejecting it.

## Inferential statistics for different types of data

### Frequencies

In the case of distributions, we are almost bound to be concerned with measures of agreement: does the distribution conform to some theoretical prediction? In the case of contingency tables we may likewise want to evaluate agreement with a theoretical prediction, but are more likely to want to test independence. In the latter case, we see if the distribution on one variable is different for different values of another variable. Significance tests assess the probability of obtaining the results under either of these hypotheses.

49

A style of significance testing found in all basic texts calculates a statistic called $\chi^2$ (Chi-squared) which is found by applying the formula

$$\chi^2 = \Sigma \ \frac{(O - E)^2}{E}$$

where $E$ is the expected frequency of occurrence if the null hypothesis is true, $O$ is the frequency actually observed, and $\Sigma$ is an instruction to carry out the calculation for each pair of frequencies (one observed and one expected) and sum the results.

The calculations are easy and the main problem is to decide on the expected frequencies, $E$, that correspond to the null hypothesis under test. Validity of the answers depends on certain conditions being met, principally independence of the scores and having an adequate amount of data. (Other methods allowing exact calculation of probabilities can be used if there are few observations.) It is, however, a serious error to apply these calculations to data that are not independent or not frequencies. The commonest cause of non-independence is having an individual contribute more than one unit to the count of frequencies, so it is a good rule of thumb that the total of the observed frequencies should equal the number of individuals. Another useful rule is that the total of "expected" frequencies in the calculation of any $\chi^2$ must equal the total of the "observed" frequencies.

Another style of analysis is called log-linear modelling. It is more versatile but less well known than applications of Chi-squared. There is an introduction by Upton (1986), and books by Everitt (1977) and Upton (1978).

### Univariate measures

For measurements, the most developed set of methods is called analysis of variance (ANOVA) (Iversen and Norpoth, 1987). It differs from other methods mainly in complexity. For example, it allows one to test the existence of several different effects in the same set of data simultaneously and it can also evaluate the extent to which one effect depends on (or interacts with) another. The price of its versatility is that it can be trusted only when certain assumptions are met, but these assumptions are not very restrictive; in any case it is often possible to transform data before analysis so as to conform better to the requirements of ANOVA. A version of ANOVA for comparing just two sets of scores, called the *t*-test, was one of the first significance tests to become known in psychology and has been very prominent ever since. Because of its versatility, several efficient types of experimental designs have been developed specifically with a view to analysis by ANOVA.

### Bivariate measures

The correlation coefficient (*r*), discussed as a descriptive technique for bivariate data, is conceptually related to ANOVA and the square of $r$ estimates the proportion of variance in one variable that can be predicted from knowledge of the other. It is not a test of significance, but its significance can be tested. Our calculated $r$ is a description of the data, but we can use a form of ANOVA or $t$-test to ask if the true value of $r$ in the population we are sampling from might plausibly be zero. We can also ask if two values of $r$ obtained from different samples might plausibly have been drawn from populations having the same value of $r$ by means of Fisher's $z$ transform.

If we want to know whether the relationship between two variables is or is not linear, we must not merely look for a significant linear relationship. A curved relationship usually contains a linear relationship, as in Figure 3c, so that $r$ is not zero. The linear component of a curved relationship may be highly significant, so a significant linear component does not demonstrate absence of curvature. If a curved line fits significantly better than a straight one, we have shown that the relationship is curved, not straight. Unfortunately, that does not work in reverse – we can never prove that a straight line is the best description of the data because allowing curvature *always* improves the fit! But if we can show that the improvement in fit is no more than would be expected by chance we can conclude that a linear relationship is an adequate description. We can also calculate confidence intervals for the amount of curvature present.

## Multivariate measures

When data are multivariate, quite different analyses are required. The essential problem is that the number of possible *patterns* increases rapidly when the number of measures increases. Even if responses are only "yes" and "no", there are over a thousand possible patterns from ten questions and over a million patterns with only twenty questions. If all of these patterns potentially mean different things, it is difficult to obtain enough data to sample them adequately. Furthermore, it is difficult or impossible to *represent* them in any way that can be comprehended, so we must summarize the results drastically.

Among the possible multivariate analyses are discriminant analysis, multivariate analysts of variance (MANOVA), principal components analysis (PCA), and factor analysis. The one general principle that I shall state is that it is almost always invalid to embark on a multivariate analysis unless the number of individuals is substantially greater than the number of components in each multivariate measure. I shall not offer any detailed guidance but just give an alert to the nature of multivariate data and the need to seek advice if you want to analyse it in any way that needs a computer. As a first step, you could consult Harris (1985) or Tabachnick and Fidell (1989).

## Nonparametric statistics

All significance tests propose a "statistical model" to explain the observed data and evaluate the probability of obtaining such results if the model is valid. The methods described so far are parametric methods because they determine which elements (parameters) of the model are needed to explain the data. When a new parameter is included the model always fits better and the test determines if the improvement is more than would be expected by chance. If so, we can conclude that the parameter is needed for a good explanation of the data. Bradley (1968), Leach (1979), Mosteller and Rourke (1973), and others recommend the use of nonparametric methods in some circumstances, because we cannot always be confident that the models invoked by parametric methods are justified. Essentially, what they argue for is not specifically *nonparametric* methods but robust or distribution-free methods – what Mosteller and Rourke call "sturdy statistics", whose answers do not depend much on assumptions.

Individual values departing considerably from the rest of the data can have a marked effect on some statistical calculations. Such exceptional scores sometimes have different origins from the others with which they have been grouped and may be considered to be outliers, that is, scores that do not properly belong with the others. If so, it is usually best to treat each as a special case and omit it from the calculation. There are no firm rules for identifying outliers, but see Lovie (1986) and Tukey (1977).

Another possibility is to replace each score by its rank, so that out of $N$ scores, the smallest has rank 1 and the largest has rank $N$. Methods using ranks can be used for descriptive and inferential statistics and are not much affected by outliers among the original scores. The best known rank methods lack the ability of ANOVA and its relatives to deal in an integrated way with very complex data, but if your data and questions are appropriate, rank methods may serve your needs well, as Meddis (1984) shows. A product-moment correlation calculated from ranks is called a Spearman correlation, whose symbol is $\rho$ (the Greek letter rho).

Since the early 1980s there has been expansion in nonparametric methods based on a technique called randomization (Edgington, 1980) which usually requires a computer but can achieve something like the versatility of ANOVA without its assumptions.

## Directional and non-directional tests

When only two groups are being compared, there are three different null hypotheses we might consider when trying to reach a conclusion about the populations the groups are drawn from. One is that there is no difference between the populations, with the alternative hypothesis that there is some difference (in either direction). If we test that one, we have a non-directional test, also called a two-tailed test. A second null hypothesis is that Population *A* scores at least as high as Population *B*, with the alternative hypothesis that Population *B* scores higher than Population *A*. The third is like the second, but transposing *A* and *B*. These are directional or one-tailed tests. A given size of difference in a directional test results in a smaller probability of occurrence by chance than in a non-directional test if the outcome is in the direction implied by the alternative hypothesis. If it is in the opposite direction, the same size of difference gives no reason to reject the null hypothesis so the result is not significant. It is often said that in order to use a directional test we need to predict the direction of the difference before observing the data. But in fact, that is not sufficient. To invoke a directional null hypothesis, we must be prepared to say that any outcome in the direction opposite to the one predicted will be interpreted as a chance result, *however great the effect turns out to be.*

### Multiple comparisons: planned and unplanned

It is not valid to apply a method designed to compare two sets of scores to a situation where there are really several sets. If you measure two groups on twenty independent attributes you should not be surprised if one of the comparisons reaches the .05 level of significance — you expect one case in twenty to reach it by chance alone. If you intend to make twenty comparisons you must test a null hypothesis that takes account of that intention.

For the example just stated the procedure might be multivariate, but the problem can arise with univariate data too. Suppose you have completed an experiment with four different conditions and have carried out an ANOVA which has not proved significant. Nevertheless you observe that condition 2 has resulted in generally low scores while condition 4 has produced high ones. You compare conditions 2 and 4 using a *t*-test and find that the difference *is* significant. What has gone wrong?

The problem is that if you have two sets of data, as supposed by the *t*-test, there is only one comparison that can be made and the test tells you the probability of obtaining such results from that comparison. When you have four sets of data, there are six pairs you might consider: 1–2, 1–3, 1–4, 2–3, 2–4, and 3–4. The probability that at least one out of these six comparisons will produce such results by chance is clearly higher than the probability that one particular comparison will do so. Thus the result is more likely than the *t*-test suggests and the result is not really significant.

The situation may be even worse, because there are yet other comparisons such as $1 - (2 + 3)$ or $1 - (2 + 3 + 4)$. A technique that evaluates a true significance level where all possible comparisons can be considered is the Scheffé test. If you are not interested in comparing groups of conditions with others but only pairs of single conditions, the Scheffé test is much too cautious. Tests such as Newman-Keuls, Duncan, and Tukey can be used instead.

53

Dunnett's test is appropriate if all the comparisons are with a single condition, for example if four experimental groups are each compared with the same control group. Hsu's test can be used if you want to discover if one out of a set of conditions is significantly better (or worse) than all of the others. These and other multiple comparison tests are explained in statistical textbooks such as those of Howell (1989) and Iversen and Norpoth (1987).

The situation is different again if you know before looking at the data that you will be interested in particular comparisons. Provided that the comparisons are orthogonal (the outcome of one does not help us to predict another) the significance given by a standard test, such as a $t$-test, can be interpreted without adjustment, in fact ANOVA can be thought of as a set of such planned comparisons. The essential difference is between comparisons selected on the basis of the data and comparisons selected on the basis of the design of the investigation. In the former case, if the data had turned out differently, other comparisons would have been made, giving other ways of obtaining a result of the size you have, whereas in the latter case there is only one way to obtain it.

## PARAMETER ESTIMATION AND CONFIDENCE INTERVALS

There is a regrettable tendency in psychological statistics to focus on the *significance* of results rather than on their *importance* – a distinction nicely captured by Bolles (1962). It is true that unless you have managed to demonstrate significance (cast doubt on chance as an explanation for your results) it will be difficult to get others to take them seriously. However, your results may be highly significant and yet not important, even if the topic is an important one. The reason is that with a large amount of data, significance can be demonstrated even for a very weak effect. Thus in addition to significance, we must pay attention to magnitude of effect (see especially Cohen, 1977; Howell, 1987). Various measures have been devised to describe the magnitude of effects, but an appealing one is the proposal by Levy (1967) to characterize an effect in terms of the proportion of individuals who are correctly classified if the effect is used for the sorting.

The descriptive approach called parameter estimation focuses on the size of effect rather than on significance. Parameters are hypothetical characteristics of the population and they are estimated from the data. Parameter estimates should not change systematically as the sample size changes but significance does. It is the parameter estimates that show the *importance* of an effect, because they describe the differences among the sets of scores being compared. The degree of success in deducing group membership from scores depends on these differences and not on the *significance* of the effect.

A confidence interval is a hybrid of a descriptive statistic and a significance test. The idea is that when you estimate a parameter, for example a population mean or correlation, you also calculate a range of values (a confidence interval) within which you are reasonably confident that its true value lies. (There is no uncertainty about the mean of your sample of data but you are uncertain about the mean of the population.) If you have a large amount of consistent data, the interval will be narrow and you will be sure of the value of the measure. If you have less data, or if the results are less consistent, the interval will be wider and you will be more uncertain about the true value of the measure.

Confidence intervals are particularly useful if your purpose is to show that treatments or groups do not differ. If the confidence interval for an estimate of the true difference includes zero, the upper and lower bounds estimate respectively the largest positive and negative difference that can reasonably exist. If the data are consistent and plentiful, the interval will be narrow so any difference between the treatments must be small.

As with tests of significance, the answer is not definite but acknowledges that there is a finite probability of error. The upper bound of the .95 confidence interval is that value for the population parameter which, if it were the true value, would allow by chance an estimate at least as *low* as that obtained on 2.5 per cent of occasions. The lower bound is the value which would allow a result at least as *high* as the one observed on 2.5 per cent of occasions.

Confidence intervals are described in the better textbooks of psychological statistics, but less prominently than significance tests. When they are discussed it is usually in connection with ANOVA, perhaps because these are the easiest confidence intervals to calculate, but they can be calculated for virtually any statistical result, such as a correlation coefficient or an estimate of the proportion of people who answer a question in a certain way.

## FURTHER READING

Ferguson, G. A., & Takane, Y. (1989). *Statistical analysis in psychology and education* (6th edn). New York: McGraw-Hill

Hays, W. L. (1988). *Statistics* (4th edn). New York: Holt, Rinehart & Winston.

Hoaglin, D. C., Mosteller, F., & Tukey, J. W. (Eds) (1983). *Understanding robust and exploratory data analysis*. Chichester: Wiley.

Howell, D. C. (1989). *Fundamental statistics for the behavioral sciences* (2nd edn). Boston, MA: PWS-Kent.

Pagano, R. R. (1990). *Understanding statistics in the behavioural sciences* (3rd edn). St Paul, MN: West.

## REFERENCES

Bolles, R. C. (1962). The difference between statistical hypotheses and scientific hypotheses. *Psychological Reports*, *11*, 639–645.

Bradley, J. V. (1968). Distribution-free statistical tests. Englewood Cliffs, NJ: Prentice-Hall.

Chernoff, H. (1973). The use of faces to represent points in k-dimensional space graphically. *Journal of the American Statistical Association*, *68*, 361–368.

Cleveland, W. S. (1985). *The elements of graphing data*. Monterey, CA: Wadsworth.
Cleveland, W. S., & McGill, R. (1985). Graphical perception and graphical methods for analyzing scientific data. *Science, 229*, 828.
Cohen, J. (1977). *Statistical power analysis for the behavioral sciences*. New York: Academic Press.
Edgington, E. S. (1980). Randomization tests. New York: Marcel Dekker.
Everitt, B. S. (1977). *The analysis of contingency tables*. London: Chapman & Hall.
Everitt, B. S. (1978). *Graphical techniques for multivariate data*. London: Heinemann.
Harris, R. J. (1985). *A primer of multivariate statistics* (2nd edn). New York: Academic Press.
Howell, D. C. (1987). *Statistical methods for psychology* (2nd edn). Boston, MA: Duxbury.
Howell, D. C. (1989). *Fundamental statistics for the behavioral sciences* (2nd edn). Boston, MA: PWS-Kent.
Iversen, G. R., & Norpoth, H. (1987). *Analysis of variance* (2nd edn) Newbury Park, CA: Sage.
Leach, C. (1979). *Introduction to statistics: A nonparametric approach for the social sciences*. Chichester: Wiley.
Levy, P. M. (1967). Substantive significance of significant differences between two groups. *Psychological Bulletin, 67*, 37–40.
Levy, P. M. (1981). On the relation between method and substance in psychology. *Bulletin of the British Psychological Society, 34*, 265–270.
Lovie, P. (1986). Identifying outliers. In A. D. Lovie (Ed.) *New developments in statistics for psychology and the social sciences* (pp. 44–69). London: British Psychological Society/Routledge.
McGuigan, F. J. (1983). *Experimental psychology: Methods of research* (4th edn). Englewood Cliffs, NJ: Prentice-Hall.
MacRae, A. W. (1988). Measurement scales and statistics: What can significance tests tell us about the world? *British Journal of Psychology, 79*, 161–171.
Meddis, R. (1984). *Statistics using ranks: A unified approach*. Oxford: Basil Blackwell.
Mosteller, F., & Rourke, R. E. K. (1973). *Sturdy statistics: Nonparametrics and order statistics*. Reading, MA: Addison-Wesley.
Phillips, L. D. (1973). *Bayesian statistics for social scientists*. London: Nelson.
Rouanet, H., & Lecoutre, B. (1983). Specific inference in ANOVA: From significance tests to Bayesian procedures. *British Journal of Mathematical and Statistical Psychology, 36*, 252–268.
Rouanet, H., Lépine, D., & Pelnard-Considère, J. (1976). Bayes-fiducial procedures as practical substitutes for misplaced significance testing: An application to educational data. In D. N. M. de Gruijter & L. J. Th. van der Kamp (Eds) *Advances in psychological and educational measurement* (pp. 33–50). New York: Wiley.
Stevens, S. S. (1946). On the theory of scales of measurement. *Science, 103*, 677–680.
Stevens, S. S. (1951). Mathematics, measurement and psychophysics. In S. S. Stevens (Ed.) *Handbook of experimental psychology* (pp. 1–49) New York: Wiley.
Tabachnick, B. G., & Fidell, L. S. (1989). *Using multivariate statistics* (2nd edn). New York: Harper & Row.
Tufte, E. R. (1983). *The visual display of quantitative information*. Cheshire, CT: Graphics Press.
Tukey, J. W. (1977). *Exploratory data analysis*. Reading, MA: Addison-Wesley.
Upton, G. J. G. (1978). *The analysis of cross-tabulated data*. Chichester: Wiley.

Upton, G. J. G. (1986). Cross-classified data. In A. D. Lovie (Ed.) *New developments in statistics for psychology and the social sciences* (pp. 70–92). Leicester: British Psychological Society.

Wainer, H., & Thissen, D. (1981). Graphical data analysis. *Annual Review of Psychology*, *32*, 191–241.

# 4

# QUASI-EXPERIMENTS AND CORRELATIONAL STUDIES

*Michael L. Raulin and Anthony M. Graziano*
State University of New York at Buffalo, USA

| | |
|---|---|
| **Experimental research** | **Correlational approaches** |
| **Quasi-experimental procedures** | Simple correlations |
| Non-equivalent control-group designs | Advanced correlational techniques |
| Differential research designs | Simple linear regression |
| Interrupted time-series designs | Advanced regression techniques |
| Single-subject designs | Path analysis |
| Reversal (ABA) design | **Conclusion** |
| Multiple baseline design | **Further reading** |
| Single-subject, randomized, time-series design | **References** |

Scientific research is a process of inquiry – sequences of asking and answering questions about the nature of relationships among variables (e.g., How does *A* affect *B*? Do *A* and *B* vary together? Is *A* significantly different from *B*? and so on). Scientific research is carried out at many levels that differ in the types of questions asked and, therefore, in the procedures used to answer them. Thus, the choice of which methods to use in research is largely determined by the kinds of questions that are asked.

In research, there are four basic questions about the relationships among variables: causality, differences between groups, direction and strength of relationships, and contingencies. This chapter will focus primarily on three of them: methods applied to questions of causality (experiments and quasi-experiments), methods to address questions about group differences (differential research), and methods used to answer questions about the direction and strength of relationships among variables (correlations). (For more detail on these topics see Graziano and Raulin, 1993.)

## EXPERIMENTAL RESEARCH

Experiments are the most effective way to address questions of causality — does one variable have an effect upon another (e.g., Does a new drug $X$ reduce anxiety?). A precise and well-controlled experiment eliminates alternative explanations of results. If a well-designed experiment indicates that anxiety decreases when drug $X$ is given, we shall have high confidence that it was drug $X$, and not some other factor, that brought about the decrease.

In an experiment, the causal hypothesis (that $X$, the independent variable, will affect $Y$, the dependent variable) is tested by manipulating $X$ and observing $Y$. In the simplest experiment, the independent variable is manipulated by presenting it to one group of subjects and not presenting it to another group. The two groups must be comparable prior to the manipulation so that any post-manipulation group difference is clearly due to the independent variable and not to some other, extraneous variable. If an uncontrolled, extraneous variable may have affected the outcome, then we have an alternative explanation of the results. Consequently, we cannot be sure which variables were actually responsible for the effects. Comparability of groups before the manipulation is assured by assigning subjects randomly to the groups.

Well-designed experiments have sufficient controls to eliminate alternative explanations, allowing us to draw causal conclusions. Uncontrolled variables threaten the validity of the experiment and our conclusions. For example, suppose you develop a headache while working for hours at your computer. You stop, go into another room, and take two aspirin. After about 15 minutes your headache is gone and you return to work. Like most people, you would probably conclude that the aspirin eliminated the headache, that is, you would infer a causal relationship between variable $X$ (aspirin) and variable $Y$ (headache). But other variables besides the aspirin might have been responsible for the improvement. You stopped working for awhile. You left the room and stretched your legs. You may have closed your eyes for a few minutes and rubbed your temples. You took a cool drink of water when you swallowed the aspirin. Mostly, you took a break from the intensive work and relaxed for a few minutes. All of those variables are potential contributors to the observed effect; they are confounding factors in the research. Therefore, it is not clear that it was the aspirin alone that reduced the headache. To be confident of a causal relationship between the aspirin and headache reduction, one would have to carry out an experiment designed to control these confounding factors and to eliminate the alternative explanations.

The discussion above refers to one of the most important concepts in experimentation – validity. A research study has good validity when it controls confounding factors and thus eliminates rival explanations, allowing a causal conclusion. To state it another way, uncontrolled extraneous variables threaten the validity of experiments.

## QUASI-EXPERIMENTAL PROCEDURES

Experiments allow us to draw causal inferences with the greatest confidence. However, there are conditions under which we cannot meet all demands of a true experiment but still want to address causal questions. In these situations we can use quasi-experimental designs. Using quasi-experiments in clinical and field situations to draw cautious causal inferences is preferable to not experimenting at all.

Quasi-experimental designs resemble experiments but are weak on some of the characteristics. Quasi-experiments include a comparison of at least two levels of an independent variable, but the manipulation is not always under the experimenter's control. For example, suppose we are interested in the health effects of a natural disaster such as a destructive tornado. We cannot manipulate the tornado but we can compare those who experienced the tornado with a group of people who did not. Likewise, in many field situations we cannot assign subjects to groups in an unbiased manner. Indeed, we often cannot assign subjects at all, but must accept the natural groups as they exist. Thus, in quasi-experimental designs:

1 We state a causal hypothesis.
2 We include at least two levels of the independent variable, although we may not manipulate it.
3 We usually cannot assign subjects to groups, but must accept existing groups.
4 We include specific procedures for testing hypotheses.
5 We include some controls for threats to validity.

Compare this list with the characteristics of a *true* experiment:

1 We state a causal hypothesis.
2 We manipulate the independent variable.
3 We assign subjects randomly to groups.
4 We use systematic procedures to test the hypothesized causal relationships.
5 We use specific controls to reduce threats to validity.

There are a number of basic quasi-experimental designs, but we shall focus on four of the most important: non-equivalent control-group designs, differential research designs, interrupted time-series designs, and single-subject designs.

## Non-equivalent control-group designs

We can test causal hypotheses with confidence if we randomly assign subjects to groups, because such groups are likely to be equivalent at the beginning of the study. However, sometimes subjects cannot be assigned randomly to groups, and the groups may not be equivalent on some variables at the beginning of the study. Campbell and Stanley (1966) popularized the non-equivalent control-group design by suggesting that already existing groups can be similar to one another on most relevant variables even though there is no systematic assignment of subjects to groups. The more similar natural groups are to one another, the closer the design approximates a true experiment. Furthermore, Cook and Campbell (1979) showed that it is sometimes possible to draw strong conclusions from non-equivalent control-group studies, even when the groups are different, provided the researcher carefully evaluates all potential threats to validity.

There are two problems with non-equivalent groups: groups may be different on the dependent measure(s) at the start of the study, and there may be other differences between groups. To address the first issue, we include a pre-test measure. The pre-test tells us how similar the groups are on the dependent variable(s) at the beginning of the study. The more similar the groups are, the greater control we have. To address the second issue − that groups may differ on variables other than the dependent variable − it is important to rule out each potential confounding variable. To do this, we must first identify potential confounding variables, measure them, and carefully rule them out. Figure 1 shows six possible outcomes of a non-equivalent control-group design. In Figures 1(a), 1(b), and 1(c) the pattern of scores for the experimental and control groups suggests no effect of the independent variable. In Figure 1(a), neither group changes; the pre-test scores suggest that the group differences existed prior to the independent variable manipulation. Both Figures 1(b) and 1(c) show an equivalent increase in the groups on the dependent measure from pre-test to post-test, suggesting that there is no effect of the independent variable. Again, the pre-test in 1(b) allows us to rule out the hypothesis that the group post-test differences are due to the independent variable. In Figure 1(d), groups equivalent at the beginning of the study diverge; there does appear to be an effect of the independent variable. In both Figures 1(e) and 1(f), the groups differ on the dependent measure at pre-test, and the experimental group changes more than the control group after the manipulation. Figure 1(f) shows a slight change in the control group but a marked change in the experimental group, suggesting an effect of the independent variable. However, there is still the potentially confounding factor of regression to the mean. Regression is a potential source of confounding whenever we begin an experiment with extreme scores. The marked pre-test difference between groups in Figure 1(f) may represent extreme scores for the experimental group. In the course of the experiment the scores for the group may have returned to the mean level represented by the control group. Consequently, we cannot be confident in attributing the results to the causal effects of the independent variable. In Figure 1(e), the control group does not change but the experimental group changes markedly in the predicted direction, even going far beyond the level of the control group. This is called a crossover effect. The results give us considerable confidence in a causal inference. Maturation (normal changes in subjects over time) and history (changes in subjects during the study due to events other than the independent variable manipulation) are unlikely alternative hypotheses because the control group should also have been affected by these factors. Regression to the mean is also an unlikely alternative hypothesis because the experimental group increased not only to the mean of the control group but also beyond it. With these results a quasi-experimental design gives us fairly good confidence in a causal inference.

These examples are reasonably interpretable. Other situations described by Cook and Campbell (1979) are more difficult, or even impossible, to

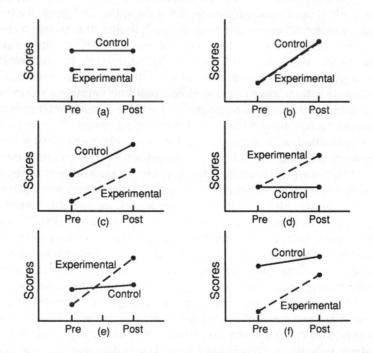

*Figure 1*  Possible outcomes from non-equivalent control group studies

interpret. Using non-equivalent control group designs appropriately requires considerable expertise.

## Differential research designs

In differential research, pre-existing groups (e.g., diagnostic groups) are compared on one or more dependent measures. There is no random assignment to groups; subjects are classified into groups and measured on the dependent variable. In essence, the researcher measures two variables (the variable defining the group and the dependent variable). Consequently, many researchers classify differential research as a variation of correlational research. We believe that differential research designs can employ control procedures not available in straight correlational research and therefore should be conceptualized as somewhere between quasi-experimental and correlational designs. We cannot draw causal conclusions from differential research, but we can test for differences between groups.

A typical differential research study might compare depressed and non-depressed subjects. The dependent variable is selected for its theoretical significance. For example, we might measure people's judgment of the probability of succeeding on a test of skill, as Alloy and Abramson (1979) did. They hypothesized that depressed subjects would be more likely to expect failure. This hypothesis was based on a causal model of depression that suggested that one's attributional style would affect the risk for depression. This causal model could not be tested directly with a differential research design, but the data from this study could test the plausibility of the model. If there were attributional differences in depressed and non-depressed subjects, then it is plausible that these differences predated the depression, perhaps even contributing to the development of depression.

One could think of a differential research study as including an implicit manipulation that occurs prior to data collection – a manipulation that created the defining characteristic of the groups. This would be equivalent to comparing a group of people who lived through a tornado and a group who had never experienced one. The groups are defined by an event that predated the research study. However, the exposure to a tornado is likely a random event, so this comparison is conceptually close to an experiment. The subjects are assigned randomly, although not by the researcher; one group experiences the independent variable (i.e., the tornado), although again not controlled by the researcher; dependent measures are taken after the manipulation. We would classify such a study as a strong quasi-experimental design and would feel justified in drawing rather strong causal conclusions on the basis of our group comparisons. However, when the manipulation is something less likely to be random, such as becoming depressed or not, the possibility of confounding is greatly increased.

Whenever you start with pre-existing groups, the groups are likely to differ on many variables other than the variable that defines the groups. For example, if we compare schizophrenic patients with a randomly selected non-patient control sample, the groups would differ not only on diagnosis, but probably also on social class, education level, average IQ, amount of hospitalization, history of medication use, and the social stigma associated with a psychiatric diagnosis. Any difference between our schizophrenic and control samples could be due to the disease or any of the other differences listed above. These variables are all confounded with the diagnosis of the subjects. It is impossible to draw a strong conclusion.

Confounding is the norm in differential research, even in cases where you might not expect it. For example, if we compare children of various ages in a cross-sectional developmental study, we might expect that the children made it into the various groups by the random factor of when they were born. That may be true, but there are likely to be differences between the groups that are a function of historical factors unique to a given age range of children. These might include major historical events occurring at critical ages, differences in economic conditions that affect what resources are available to the children at any given age, differences in school systems that may be the result of budget issues or political pressures, or even the impact of a single teacher. (Note that most samples of subjects for research come from accessible populations from a narrow geographic area. Therefore, it is possible that a single teacher could differentially affect the results.) Differences between age groups that are the result of a different set of historical experiences are known as cohort effects.

The ideal control group in differential research is identical to the experimental group on everything except the variable that defines the groups. This ideal often is impossible. Therefore, researchers attempt to equate the groups on critical variables, that is, variables that could confound the interpretation of the results. A variable can confound the results, first, if it has an effect on the dependent variable, and second, if there is a mean difference on the variable in the groups being compared. For example, IQ might confound results in a study of cognitive styles, but hair colour is unlikely to because hair colour is probably unrelated to cognitive styles. However, even though IQ is a potential confounding variable, it cannot confound the results *unless* there is a mean difference between the groups. In differential research, it is common to include control groups that are matched on one or more of these critical variables to avoid confounding. For more discussion of this strategy, see Chapman and Chapman (1973) and Graziano and Raulin (1993).

## Interrupted time-series designs

In interrupted time-series designs, a single group of subjects is measured several times both before and after some event or manipulation. The multiple measures over time strengthen the design considerably over a simple pre-post design, controlling many potential confounding factors. A major potential confounding factor in the simple pre-post study is regression to the mean. Behaviour fluctuates over time, displaying considerable variability. The intervention might be applied only at a high point in that natural variation, just before the behaviour decreased again. Thus, the observed changes in behaviour may not be due to the treatment at all but only to the natural variability of behaviour. The same reduction might have been observed even if we had not applied the treatment. The multiple measures of the interrupted time-series design give several points of comparison, allowing us to rule out the effects of regression to the mean. We can see the natural variability and can see if the post-treatment change exceeds the natural variability.

Figure 2 shows the results of an interrupted time-series study of disruption in autistic children (Graziano, 1974). Disruptive behaviour of four autistic children was monitored for a full year before the treatment (relaxation training) was introduced and a year following the treatment. Note that the variability during baseline disappears after treatment, with disruptive behaviour dropping to zero and remaining there for a full year. Such results are not likely due to normal fluctuation or regression to the mean. They also seem unlikely to be due to maturation of all subjects during the same period of time. With time-series designs, however, there are still two potentially confounding factors – history and instrumentation. History can confound results in any procedure that requires a fairly long period of time because other events might account for changes in the dependent variable. Thus, when using the interrupted time-series design, the experimenter must identify potential confounding due to history and carefully rule it out. Instrumentation is another potential threat to validity. When new programmes are started there may be accompanying changes in the way records are kept. The

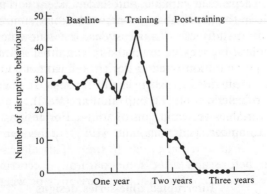

*Figure 2* An interrupted time-series design showing the effects of relaxation treatment on disruptive behaviour in autistic children

researcher must be careful to determine that an apparent change is not due to changes in record-keeping.

The interrupted time-series design is useful in clinical or naturalistic settings where the effects of some event, naturally occurring or manipulated, can be assessed by taking multiple measurements both before and after the event. It can also be used in studies where the presumed causal event occurs to all members of a population. For example, the effects of a policy change (e.g., a change in the speed limit) could be evaluated with an interrupted time-series design using routinely gathered data (e.g., traffic fatality counts).

The interrupted time-series design can be improved by adding one or more comparison groups. In our hypothetical study of the effects of a change in speed limit on the number of fatalities, we could use comparable data from a neighbouring state that did not reduce the speed limit. Such a comparison would help to control for potentially confounding factors such as history and maturation.

Graphical presentations of data in the interrupted time-series design can provide considerable information. In a time-series study, the change in the time graph must be sharp to be interpreted as anything other than only a normal fluctuation. Slight or gradual changes are difficult to interpret. But in a time-series design, simply inspecting the graph is not enough. Testing the statistical significance of pre-post differences in time-series designs requires sophisticated procedures, which are beyond the scope of this chapter (see Glass, Willson, & Gottman, 1975; or Kazdin, 1992).

## Single-subject designs

Single-subject designs were developed early in the history of experimental psychology and were used in both human and animal learning studies. Since the early 1960s they have become popular in clinical psychology. With single-subject designs we are able to manipulate independent variables, to observe their effects on dependent variables, to draw causal inferences, and to do so with a single subject. Modern clinical psychology is now heavily reliant on behaviour modification treatment methods, and behaviour modification research utilizes single-subject research designs refined from the work of B. F. Skinner. For more information on single-subject designs, consult Barlow and Hersen (1984), Kratochwill (1978), and Sidman (1960).

Single-subject designs are variations of time-series designs. The same subject is exposed to all manipulations, and we take dependent measurements of the same subject at different points in time. This allows us to compare measures taken before and after some naturally occurring event or an experimental manipulation. The basic comparison is between the same subject's own pre-treatment and post-treatment responses. Note that at its simplest level, this resembles the pre-test–post-test comparison – a relatively weak non-experimental design. A control group would strengthen a pre-test

– post-test design, but a control group is not possible when we have only one subject. Single-subject designs improve on the pre-post design, not by adding a control group, but by adding more conditions to the experiment. If the dependent variable changes in the predicted direction at each manipulation, we can have reasonable confidence that the manipulation is responsible for the observed change in the dependent variable. There are several single-subject designs, including reversal or ABA designs, multiple baseline designs, and single-subject, randomized, time-series designs.

## Reversal (ABA) design

In reversal or ABA designs, the effects of an independent variable on a dependent variable are demonstrated by measuring the dependent variable at three or four points in time. There is a no-treatment baseline period during which the dependent behaviour is only observed, a treatment period in which the manipulation is carried out, and a return or reversal to the no-treatment condition. The effects of the independent variable (the treatment) on the dependent variable (the behaviour to be changed) is demonstrated if the behaviour changes in the predicted direction whenever the conditions are reversed. We often strengthen the design by measuring the dependent variable several times during each condition. A hypothetical study will help to describe the general format used. The study concerns self-stimulatory behaviour of a retarded child, Terry. After observing Terry in the classroom, a psychologist forms the tentative hypothesis that the teacher's attention is reinforcing the self-stimulatory behaviour. That is, whenever Terry begins her self-stimulatory activity, the teacher tries to soothe and comfort her. The teacher does not realize that it may be her efforts to help Terry control the behaviour that are actually helping to maintain it.

To test the hypothesis the psychologist sets up an ABA design, in which condition *A*, the baseline, involves the teacher's usual approach of attending to Terry whenever she displays the self-stimulatory behaviour. Condition *B* is the treatment – a differential reinforcement procedure in which the teacher provides attention and support for Terry whenever she refrains from the self-stimulatory behaviour, but withdraws attention when Terry engages in self-stipulatory behaviour. Precise observations are carried out for one hour at the same time each day. The graph in Figure 3 shows the behavioural changes as the *A* and *B* conditions are sequentially reversed. The graph suggests that there may be a causal relationship between teacher attention and Terry's self-stimulatory behaviour. Notice that the psychologist has not limited the approach to only three conditions, ABA, but has added another reversal at the end for an ABAB procedure. The ABA sequence is sufficient to suggest causality, but the demonstration of a casual link creates an ethical demand to return Terry to the optimal state.

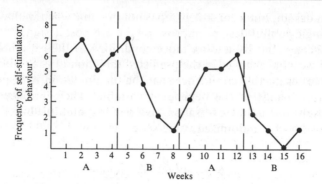

*Figure 3*  A reversal design showing the effects of contingent reinforcement on self-stimulatory behaviour of a single child

## Multiple baseline design

Although the ABA design can provide a powerful demonstration of the effect of one variable on another, there are situations in which reversal procedures are not feasible or ethical. For example, suppose in our example of Terry above, the self-stimulatory behaviour was injurious, such as severe head-banging. We would be unwilling to reverse conditions once we achieved improved functioning because it could risk injury. Instead, we could use a multiple baseline design.

In the multiple baseline design, the effects of the treatment are demonstrated on different behaviours successively. To illustrate, we shall use an example similar to the previous example. Suppose that a fifth-grade boy (about 10 years old) is doing poorly in school, although he appears to have the ability to achieve at a high level. He also disrupts class frequently and often fights with other students. A psychologist spends several hours observing the class and notes some apparent contingencies regarding the boy's behaviour. The teacher, attempting to control the boy, pays more attention to him when he is disruptive – scolding, correcting, lecturing him, and making him stand in a corner whenever he is caught fighting. The psychologist notes that the boy seems to enjoy the attention. However, on those rare occasions when he does his academic work quietly and well, the teacher ignores him completely. "When he is working, I leave well enough alone," the teacher says. "I don't want to risk stirring him up." Based on these observed contingencies, the psychologist forms the tentative hypothesis that the contingent teacher attention to the boy's disruptive behaviour and fighting may be a major factor in maintaining these behaviours, whereas the teacher's failure to reward the boy's good academic work may account for its low occurrence. The psychologist sets up a multiple-baseline design to test the hypothesis about the importance of teacher attention on disruptive

68

behaviour, fighting, and academic performance. The independent variable here is teacher attention.

Figure 4 shows the sequence of phases of the hypothetical study. During Phase 1 all three dependent variables are measured while the teacher continues the usual procedure of trying to punish the disruption and fighting while ignoring the positive academic behaviour. As seen in Figure 4, disruptive behaviour and fighting are high and academic performance is low. In Phase 2, the teacher's attention to fighting is withdrawn and positive attention is made contingent on academic work. In Phase 3, these procedures continue and the teacher withdraws attention for disruption as well as for fighting. The measured changes in the dependent variables associated with the independent variable manipulations provide evidence for the hypothesis that contingent teacher attention is an important controlling factor in the child's behaviour.

### Single-subject, randomized, time-series design

When a reversal design is not appropriate and a multiple baseline procedure is not feasible because we want to study only one behaviour, the single-subject, randomized, time-series design can be used. This design is an interrupted time-series design for a single subject with one additional element — the randomized assignment of the manipulation in the time-series.

The single-subject, randomized, time-series design could be applied in the example above, but let us take another example. Suppose that Joey, another child in the special class, does not complete his daily work. During lesson periods, when he should be responding to a workbook lesson, Joey looks around the room or just closes his eyes and does no work. Reminders from

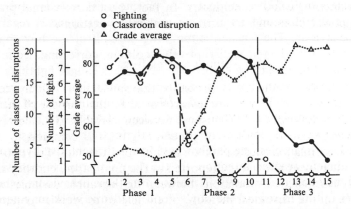

*Figure 4* A multiple baseline design showing improvement in disruptive behaviour, fighting, and academic performance for a single child contingent upon teacher attention

the teacher have little effect. An effective motivational intervention with children is a token reinforcement system in which paper or plastic tokens are given to the child whenever he engages in the desired behaviour. The tokens serve as immediate secondary reinforcement for the desired behaviour. They are saved by the child and cashed in for items and privileges. If we were to employ a single-subject, randomized, time-series design, we might decide to measure the child's homework achievement for 6 weeks (30 school days). We might decide that we want at least 5 days before and after the implementation of the treatment. This ensures adequate pre-treatment and post-treatment measures. We then use a table of random numbers to select randomly one of the middle 20 days as our point for introducing the manipulation. The manipulation is the use of token reinforcement for homework achievement. Suppose we randomly select the ninth day as the point for introducing the token reinforcement programme. The beginning of the manipulation is preceded by 8 days of baseline measurement followed by 22 days of measurements of the dependent variable under the token reinforcement condition. If the time graph shows a marked improvement in homework achievement coincident with the ninth measurement, we have a convincing illustration of the effects of the token reinforcement. Note that it is unlikely that such marked improvement would occur by chance, or because of maturational or historical factors, at exactly the point at which we have randomly introduced the treatment.

## CORRELATIONAL APPROACHES

Like quasi-experimental designs, correlation designs are used in situations in which the manipulation of an independent variable is either impossible or unethical. Because there is no experimental manipulation, one must be cautious in drawing causal conclusions. In fact, most correlational procedures are not powerful enough to justify causal interpretations.

### Simple correlations

The correlation coefficient is probably the single most widely computed statistic in psychology. In many research studies, the purpose of the study is to produce measures of relationships between variables (i.e., correlations). Even in experimental designs or other designs, it is common to compute numerous correlation coefficients to help interpret the data. These correlation coefficients may or may not be reported in the final paper, but they are often routinely computed. Correlations between demographic variables and performance on the dependent measure often help us to identify potential confounding variables in a current study or in a future study that might be run.

The most commonly used correlation coefficient is the Pearson product-moment correlation. This coefficient is used when both variables are measured on an interval or ratio scale. A Spearman rank-order correlation is preferred if at least one of the two variables is measured on an ordinal scale. Computational procedures for either of these coefficients are readily available in almost any undergraduate statistics textbook. There are other correlation coefficients available as well, which we shall discuss shortly. The range for both the Pearson and Spearman correlations is $-1.00$ to $+1.00$. A correlation of $+1.00$ indicates a perfect positive relationship (i.e., as one variable increases the other increases by a predictable amount). A correlation of $-1.00$ indicates a perfect negative relationship (i.e., as one variable increases the other variable decreases by a predictable amount). The sign indicates the direction of the relationship and the absolute size of the correlation indicates the strength of the relationship.

Correlations are most easily visualized in a scatter plot. Each person is plotted in a coordinate system in which their location is determined by the scores on variables $X$ and $Y$. Figure 5 gives several examples of scatter plots, each indicating a particular degree of relationship. The actual product-moment correlation is indicated next to each scatter plot. Figures 5(a) and 5(b) illustrate scatter plots for strong positive and negative correlations, respectively. Figures 5(c) and 5(d) illustrate zero correlations. Note a zero correlation is often described as circular scatter plot. The scatter plot is circular, however, only if the variance on variables $X$ and $Y$ are equal, something that rarely occurs. Figure 5(d), for example, illustrates a zero correlation where variable $X$ has a greater variance than variable $Y$. In this situation, the circular correlation is elongated horizontally. Figure 5(e) shows a perfect positive relationship with all the points clearly lining up on a straight line. Figure 5(f) shows the powerful effect of a single deviant score, especially when you have a small sample. In this case, 14 of the 15 data points clearly seem to show a zero correlation, but the correlation when you include the fifteenth point (at 10, 10) is .77. Finally, scatter plots shown in Figure 5(g) and 5(h) illustrate non-linear correlations. The product-moment correlation is sensitive only to the linear component. In Figure 5(g), the correlation is essentially zero, whereas in Figure 5(h), the correlation is somewhat positive. In both Figure 5(g) and 5(h), the product-moment correlation is an inappropriate measure of relationship. Simple product-moment correlation should be used only in situations where you anticipate a linear relationship between variables $X$ and $Y$.

As mentioned earlier, the strength of the relationship between $X$ and $Y$ is illustrated by the size of the correlation regardless of the sign. A commonly used index is the square of the correlation, which can be interpreted as the proportion of variability in one variable that is predictable on the basis of knowing the scores on the second variable. This statement is usually shortened to "the proportion of variance accounted for".

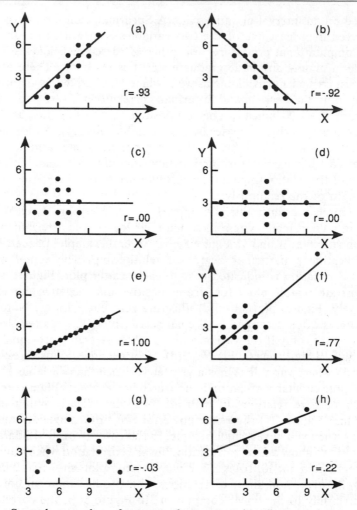

*Figure 5* Several examples of scatter plots, regression lines, and the product-moment correlations that each plot represents

## Advanced correlational techniques

More sophisticated correlational procedures are also available. You can correlate one variable with an entire set of variables (multiple correlation) or one set of variables with another set of variables (canonical correlation). It is also possible to correlate one variable with another after statistically removing the effects of a third variable (partial correlation). Discussion of these procedures is beyond the scope of this chapter, but the interested reader is referred to Nunnally (1976) for a more detailed discussion.

## Simple linear regression

Regression techniques utilize the observed relationship between two or more variables to make predictions. The simplest regression technique is linear regression, with one variable being predicted on the basis of scores on a second variable. The equation below shows the general form for the prediction equation.

Predicted $Y$ score $= (b \times X) + a$

The values of the slope $b$ and the intercept $a$ in the above equation are a function of the observed correlation and the variances for both the $X$ and $Y$ variables. The computational detail can be found in virtually any undergraduate statistics text (e.g., Shavelson, 1988). In each of the eight scatter plots shown in Figure 5, the regression line for predicting $Y$ from $X$ has been drawn. When the correlation is zero the regression line is horizontal with an intercept at the mean for $Y$. In other words, if $X$ and $Y$ are unrelated to one another the mean of the $Y$ distribution is the best prediction of $Y$, regardless of the value of $X$.

## Advanced regression techniques

It is possible to use the relationships of several variables to the variable that you wish to predict in a procedure known as multiple regression. Multiple regression is also a linear regression technique, except that instead of working in the two-dimensional space indicated in Figure 5, we are now working in $N$-dimensional space, where $N$ is equal to the number of predictor variables plus one. For example, if you have two predictor measures and one criterion measure, the prediction equation would be represented by a line in the three-dimensional space defined by these measures. If you have several predictor measures, visualizing multiple regression is difficult, even though the procedure is conceptually straightforward.

Although it is possible to put all of the predictor variables into the regression equation, it is often unnecessary to do so in order to get accurate predictions. The most commonly used procedure for a regression analysis is a procedure called stepwise regression, which uses a complex algorithm to enter variables into the equation one at a time. The algorithm starts by entering the variable that has the strongest relationship with the variable that you want to predict, and then selects additional variables on the basis of the incremental improvement in prediction that each variable provides. The computational procedures for stepwise regression are too complex to be done without the use of a statistical analysis program such as SPSS or SPSS/PC + (Norusis, 1990b).

All of the regression models discussed above assume linear regression. In Figure 5(g) and 5(h), the scatter plot suggests that there is a non-linear relationship between variables $X$ and $Y$. When a non-linear relationship exists, there are non-linear statistical procedures for fitting a curve to the data. These procedures are well beyond the scope of this chapter: the interested reader is referred to Norusis (1990a).

## Path analysis

A procedure that is rapidly becoming the standard for analysis of correlational data is path analysis. Path analysis is one of several regression procedures that fall under the general category of latent variable models. All latent variable models make the assumption that the observed data are due to a set of unobserved (i.e., latent) variables. Factor analysis is probably the most widely used of the latent variable models.

Path analysis seeks to test the viability of a specified causal model by factoring the matrix of correlations between variables within the constraints of the model. This process is best illustrated with an example. Suppose that we had three variables ($A$, $B$, and $C$) that we hypothesize are causally related to another variable ($E$). Further, we hypothesize that the causal effects of variables $B$ and $C$ on variable $E$ are indirect − that is, variables $B$ and $C$ are causally related to a variable $D$ which in turn is causally related to variable $E$. This model is illustrated in Figure 6. Straight lines in a path model represent hypothesized causal connections, while curved lines represent potential correlations that are not hypothesized to be causal. To make our example more intuitive, we shall present a scenario where such a model might make sense. We shall assume that we are studying high-risk sexual behaviour (i.e., sexual behaviour that increases the risk of HIV infection). Variable $E$ in this model is *safe-sex behaviour in heterosexual college students*. We are hypothesizing that safe-sex behaviour is a function of *knowledge of safe-sex procedures* (variable $D$) and how *vulnerable* one feels (variable $A$). Whether one obtains knowledge of safe-sex procedures is hypothesized to be a function of *whether such information is available to people* (variable $B$) and *whether one believes that AIDS is not just a disease found in gay men or IV drug users* (variable $C$). In our model, we are suggesting that simply making information about safe-sex procedures available will not lead to the practice of safe sex unless (1) the information is learned, which will occur only if (2) the person believes that heterosexual sex represents a risk. Even if the person knows about safe sex procedures, the behaviour will not be practised unless (3) the person feels vulnerable to AIDS at the time of engaging in sex. We could expand this model by adding other variables if we wanted. For example, we might hypothesize that vulnerability is increased if the person knows people with HIV infection and is temporarily decreased if the person has been drinking (i.e., additional variables $F$ and $G$ are causally related to variable $A$). However, we shall restrict our model to the five variables shown in Figure 6 to illustrate the procedures.

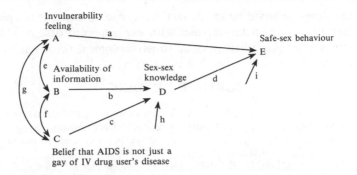

*Figure 6*  A hypothetical example of a path analysis

We have labelled the various paths in Figure 6 with lower-case letters. We shall solve for the strength of path coefficients for each of these paths. We have also included residual arrows for variables *D* and *E*. These residual arrows will have a strength that represents the unexplained variance in our model. Technically, all variables would have residual arrows, but it is customary not to include them with the initial variables (i.e., variables *A*, *B*, and *C* in our model). These variables represent our starting-point; our model does not address the question of what factors cause these initial states.

To evaluate the feasibility of our causal model, we need measures of the variables on a large sample of subjects. We need not have measures of all of the variables to do the computation; some variables may be unseen (latent). We start by computing a correlation matrix from which the path coefficients are computed. The actual path coefficient computations are beyond the scope of this chapter (the interested reader is referred to Loehlin, 1992). Path analysis tests the feasibility of a hypothesized causal model. If the absolute value of the path coefficients in the model are generally large and the residual coefficients are generally small, the model is feasible. You strive to create as parsimonious a path model as possible. Generally, as you include more paths, you will explain more of the variance, but you also run the risk of capitalizing on chance variance.

## CONCLUSION

If given a choice, a researcher should use an experimental design. Manipulating variables and observing their effects on other variables, coupled with the other controls that are a part of experimental research, gives us the greatest confidence that the observed relationship is causal. However, there are many circumstances in which experimental research is impractical or unethical. This chapter has described some of the many quasi-experimental and correlational designs available for these situations. Data from these designs should be interpreted with caution because the possibility of confounding is much larger than with experimental designs. However, these designs have proved their value in psychological research.

## FURTHER READING

Barlow, D. H., & Hersen, M. (1984). *Single case experimental designs: Strategies for studying behaviour change* (2nd edn). New York: Pergamon.

Campbell, D. T., & Stanley, J. C. (1966). *Experimental and quasi-experimental designs for research on teaching*. Chicago, IL: Rand McNally.

Cook, T. D., & Campbell, D. T. (1979). *Quasi experimentation: Design and analysis issues for field studies*. Chicago, IL: Rand McNally.

Graziano, A. M., & Raulin, M. L. (1993). *Research methods: A process of inquiry* (2nd edn). New York: Harper Collins.

Kazdin, A. E. (1992). *Research design in clinical psychology* (2nd edn). New York: Macmillan.

Loehlin, J. C. (1992). *Latent variable models: An introduction to factor, path, and structural analyses* (2nd edn). Hillsdale, NJ: Lawrence Erlbaum.

## REFERENCES

Alloy, L. B., & Abramson, L. Y. (1979). Judgment of contingencies in depressed and nondepressed subjects: Sadder but wiser? *Journal of Experimental Psychology: General, 108*, 447–485.

Barlow, D. H., & Hersen, M. (1984). *Single case experimental designs: Strategies for studying behaviour change* (2nd edn). New York: Pergamon.

Campbell, D. T., & Stanley, J. C. (1966). *Experimental and quasi-experimental designs for research on teaching*. Chicago, IL: Rand McNally.

Chapman, L. J., & Chapman, J. P. (1973). *Disordered thought in schizophrenia.* Englewood Cliffs, NJ: Prentice-Hall.

Cook, T. D., & Campbell, D. T. (1979). *Quasi experimentation: Design and analysis issues for field studies*. Chicago, IL: Rand McNally.

Glass, G. V., Willson, V. L., & Gottman, J. M. (1975). *Design and analysis of time series*. Boulder, CO: Laboratory of Educational Research Press.

Graziano, A. M. (1974). *Child without tomorrow*. Elmsford, NY: Pergamon.

Graziano, A. M., & Raulin, M. L. (1993). *Research methods: A process of inquiry* (2nd edn). New York: Harper Collins.

Kazdin, A. E. (1992). *Research design in clinical psychology* (2nd edn). New York: Macmillan.

Kratochwill, T. R. (Ed.) (1978). *Single-subject research: Strategies for evaluating change*. New York: Academic Press.

Loehlin, J. C. (1992). *Latent variable models: An introduction to factor, path, and structural analyses* (2nd edn). Hillsdale, NJ: Lawrence Erlbaum.

Norusis, M. J. (1990a). *SPSS-PC+ Advanced Statistics 4.0*. Chicago, IL: Statistical Package for the Social Sciences.

Norusis, M. J. (1990b). *SPSS-PC+ Statistics 4.0*. Chicago, IL: Statistical Package for the Social Sciences.

Nunnally, J. C. (1976). *Psychometric theory* (2nd edn). New York: McGraw-Hill.

Shavelson, R. J. (1988). *Statistical reasoning for the behavioral sciences* (2nd edn). Boston: Allyn & Bacon.

Sidman, M. (1960). *Tactics of scientific research: Evaluating scientific data in psychology*. New York: Basic Books.

# 5

# SURVEY METHODS, NATURALISTIC OBSERVATIONS, AND CASE-STUDIES

## *Francis C. Dane*
### *Mercer University, Georgia, USA*

| | |
|---|---|
| **Survey methods** | Probability sampling |
| Survey content | Non-probability sampling |
| Categorical information | **Naturalistic observation** |
| Self-reports of past | Intrusion |
| behaviour | Selecting events |
| Opinions, beliefs, attitudes, | Coding |
| and values | **Case-studies** |
| Self-reports of intentions | Sampling |
| Sensitive information | Hypothesis testing |
| Administration mode | **Further reading** |
| Sampling | **References** |

The purpose of this chapter is to provide an overview of survey methods, naturalistic observations, and case-studies as they are used in psychology. Like all research techniques, these methods are appropriate for some, but not all, research purposes. Surveys, for example, are appropriate when one wants to discover what people are willing to report about themselves and others. Naturalistic observation, in contrast, is most appropriate for monitoring the behaviour of others. Case-studies are appropriate for both of these purposes, but only when one wishes to obtain a great deal of information about one or a few people or events.

## SURVEY METHODS

Survey methods are based on the simple discovery "that asking questions is a remarkably efficient way to obtain information from and about people" (Schuman & Kalton, 1985, p. 635). The number of people may vary from a hundred to hundreds of millions, but the hallmark of surveys is that the researcher presents specific questions or items (the survey instrument) to which people (the respondents) provide answers or reactions (the responses). Thus, surveys involve an exchange of information between researcher and respondent; the researcher identifies topics of interest, and the respondent provides knowledge or opinions about those topics. Depending upon the length and content of the survey as well as the facilities available, this exchange can be accomplished via written questionnaires, in-person interviews, or telephone conversations.

In practice, the exchange of information is not always smooth. One must first decide what information is to be obtained and construct an instrument that will prompt objective responses. Questions, for example, must be phrased such that prospective respondents will understand what is being asked without introducing any bias. Then one must find the appropriate respondents and convince them to participate. Even with properly phrased questions, respondents may not know or may be unwilling to provide the requested information. Finally, depending upon the questions asked, responses may need to be coded before being analysed.

### Survey content

Traditionally, survey content has been divided into two types: fact and opinion. This dichotomy was used to acknowledge the researcher's ability to verify some information, such as age, sex, or marital status, but not other information, such as private behaviours or attitudes. Schumann & Kalton (1985), however, argued that the dichotomous distinction is overly simple and proposed the following divisions for survey content: categorical information; self-reports of past behaviour; opinions, beliefs, attitudes, and values; self-reports of intentions concerning behaviour; and sensitive information dealing with the past, present, or future. This break from the traditional, objective/subjective dichotomy reflected the increasing complexity of survey content and presaged theoretical developments concerning how people think about and report social behaviour (e.g., Fiske & Taylor, 1991). Of course, which content one includes in a specific survey instrument depends primarily upon one's research objectives. One general rule is to include only items that are relevant to the topic of interest and to avoid asking questions for which one has no explicit reason for asking.

79

## Categorical information

Surveys are an extremely efficient means by which to obtain categorical information, the dimensions that people use to describe themselves: age, education level, employment status, and so on. Although one does not always obtain accurate categorical information (Weaver & Swanson, 1974), the margin of error is generally small. There also exist attempts to establish standardized categories for use in surveys (e.g., Van Drusen & Zill, 1975). For example, Feldman (1990) used categorical information in a survey of 1,648 people employed in Denver, Colorado, to assess the concept of settlement identity – psychological bonds with the type of community in which one was raised. She used a priori response categories in which respondents were asked to categorize themselves as either a "city person", a "suburbanite", a "small-town person", or a "country/mountain" person. Additional items requested respondents to use the same categories to indicate past settlements, current settlement, and any intended future settlements.

Feldman found that the self-identification of the majority of the respondents was consistent with their history of residential experiences. For example, those who identified themselves as a "city person" were most likely to have lived in, currently lived in, and planned to continue to live in downtown areas or city neighbourhoods.

## Self-reports of past behaviour

Reports of past behaviour, too, can be easily obtained through survey methods, provided respondents understand what one is asking, can remember their past behaviour, and are willing to divulge such information. Seemingly straightforward questions are not always understood (Skogan, 1981). For example, Metts (1989) explored deception in close relationships with the question "Please describe in as much detail as possible a situation in which you were not completely truthful with [your partner]". Despite the apparent clarity of the item, about 1 per cent of the responses were too vague to be analysed. Thus, survey instruments should be pre-tested to ensure that prospective respondents will understand what is being asked of them.

Memory, too, plays a role in reporting behaviours. Survey respondents are subject to the same memory biases as other people, including the representativeness heuristic and the availability heuristic (Tversky & Kahneman, 1974, 1980). When using the former heuristic, people are more likely to report behaviours that are consistent with their self-images or stereotypes about others, while the latter heuristic involves a tendency to report more recent or more salient events. Thus, even respondents who had been victims of a crime tended to be less likely to report being victimized as the number of months between the incident and the time at which the survey was completed

80

increased (Turner, 1972). Clear instructions and an emphasis on completeness and accuracy, combined with information about why the information is being asked, appear to overcome problems related to these heuristics (Cannell, Miller, & Oksenberg, 1981).

## Opinions, beliefs, attitudes, and values

Although how one asks any question partially determines the response that one obtains, response format is particularly important when one is asking about attitudes. For example, merely being asked to provide an opinion on a given topic is sufficient to create an opinion where none existed (Fazio, Lenn, & Effrein, 1983/1984). Thus, failure to allow an explicit option for "don't know" or "no opinion" may produce inflated estimates of people's opinions by forcing them to espouse an attitude that did not exist prior to their being surveyed (Bishop, Oldendick, & Tuchfarber, 1983). Similar results have been obtained when no "neutral" response alternative is provided (Kalton, Roberts, & Holt, 1980). Respondents are likely to assume that the provided response options are the only ones in which the researcher is interested, and tailor their responses to the format presented to them.

Wording, too, is important when attempting to measure attitudes. One should always avoid double-barrelled items, which are items that contain two or more questions or statements. To do so, however, requires one to write simple items, and even seemingly trivial changes in the wording of a simple item can have a substantial impact on responses. Thus, whenever possible one should employ pre-existing measures of attitudes or pre-test a new measure to determine its level of reliability and construct validity.

## Self-reports of intentions

Reports of behavioural intentions can be understood as a combination of attitudes towards the behaviour, subjective norms or beliefs about what one is expected to do, and perceived control over the behaviour (Ajzen & Madden, 1986). Thus, to predict forthcoming behaviour one needs to determine all three aspects of intention. Although a complete discussion is beyond the scope of this chapter, research has shown that prediction is more reliable when respondents have prior experience with (Fazio & Zanna, 1981) and have more knowledge about (Kallgren & Wood, 1986) the behaviour for which intentions are stated.

Agreement between reports of intentions and completed intentions also depend upon the amount of time between the stated intention and the opportunity to engage in the behaviour (Schwartz, 1978). As the delay between the stated intention and the opportunity to fulfil it increases, the probability that the original intention will be implemented decreases. Simply put, circumstances change and greater delay allows greater change.

## Sensitive information

Any of the above types of survey content may include sensitive information – any information that, if revealed to another, would threaten a respondent's public image. Exactly what type of information may be sensitive depends, of course, on one's respondents, and preliminary research may be required to determine whether items contained in an instrument involve sensitive information. Schuman and Kalton (1985), however, argue that concern about the accuracy of responses regarding sensitive information may be overestimated because respondents tend to assume others' beliefs and behaviours are similar to their own (e.g., Ross, Greene, & House, 1977) and are therefore not reluctant to share such information.

Research on self-disclosure and privacy (e.g., Altman, 1975; Jourard, 1971) clearly indicates that one must first establish rapport with an individual before one can obtain sensitive information. Bradburn and Sudman (1979), for example, discuss a variety of strategies that can be used to increase both response rates and response accuracy when dealing with sensitive information, and all of these strategies involve gaining the trust of the respondent. Thus, tactics such as placing sensitive questions towards the end of an instrument may be effective simply because respondents, if they have cooperated to that point, have done because they already trust the researcher.

## Administration mode

One cannot state categorically that one of the three modes of survey administration – face-to-face, telephone, and mail – is better than any other in every situation. Each has its advantages and disadvantages, and each is better suited to a specific research situation.

Administering a survey through face-to-face interviewing is time-consuming and expensive, and requires well-trained interviewers. Despite the drawbacks, it remains the best mode for administering a lengthy, complicated survey instrument that contains numerous items for which responses may generate follow-up questions. Face-to-face interviews are sometimes the only way to obtain reactions to specific materials.

The proportion of residences with telephones in most industrialized countries is so high that telephone interviews may well be the most preferred survey administration mode. The ability to employ computers to dial numbers, structure questions, and immediately record responses provides additional advantages. The use of random digit dialling enables one to contact individuals with unlisted telephone numbers, and precludes the need for a priori identification of prospective respondents. With the obvious exception of presenting visual material, telephone interviews provide few disadvantages relative to personal interviews (Groves & Kahn, 1979).

Mailing instruments to respondents is the least expensive mode for a lengthy instrument, but response rates for postal surveys tend to be lower than those for telephone or personal interviews. However, when effort is expended to convince prospective respondents that the survey is worthwhile, response rates can be very high (Dillman, 1978). Enclosing monetary and other incentives also increases response rates, as do secondary and tertiary mailings for tardy respondents. The two major disadvantages to mailed surveys is that one must have a list of prospective addresses and one cannot be certain who at that address actually completed the survey.

## Sampling

Typically, one purpose of survey research is to use the results to make inferences about the probable responses of those who were not included in the group of respondents. That is, one wishes to use the sample of respondents to make predictions about the population, the group of all prospective respondents. For example, the purpose of an exit poll of voters is to predict the outcome of the election, in which case the population is all voters. Similarly, the purpose of a marketing survey is to predict consumers' responses to a new product; the population is all consumers. The extent to which survey data can be used to make such predictions validly depends upon the sampling procedures, the manner in which the actual respondents have been selected from the group of all possible respondents.

In general, there are two types of sampling procedures: probability and non-probability. Probability sampling includes all procedures for which the probability of any prospective respondent's inclusion in the sample can be estimated and is known to be non-zero. That is, every prospective respondent has at least some estimable chance of being included in the survey. Non-probability sampling includes all other procedures, that is, procedures in which some prospective respondents have a zero probability of being chosen or in which the probability of being selected cannot be estimated.

### Probability sampling

All procedures for obtaining a probability sample are, essentially, variations of placing identical slips of paper, each of which contains a name, in a hat, closing one's eyes, and plucking slips from the hat until one has the desired number of slips. This procedure is known as simple random sampling (SRS), and provides each prospective respondent with an equal chance of being selected. Thus, the key to probability sampling is the existence of a sampling frame, a list of prospective respondents (Kish, 1965). Without a sampling frame, one cannot know the number of prospective respondents, and therefore cannot determine the probability of a single respondent being selected. For example, to select a probability sample of students at University $X$ one must obtain a listing of all students enrolled at $X$.

When subgroups such as race, gender, religion, nationality, and so on, exist within the population, SRS may produce an unrepresentative sample. For example, a SRS based on geographic location might produce relatively few, if any, residents from rural areas. In such cases, stratified random sampling is the preferred procedure. Essentially, one treats each subgroup *as though* it were a population and employs SRS within the subgroups. The sub-samples selected from each subgroup are then combined to form the survey sample. The number of respondents selected from each subgroup may be proportional to their representation in the population, in which case stratified random sampling is equivalent to an ideal SRS. For a variety of reasons, however, a disproportionate stratified sample may be preferable. If the number of rural residents in the population is relatively small, one may need to select a disproportionately large sample of rural residents to obtain reliable estimates of the opinions of the population of rural residents.

Stratified sampling procedures are used to increase the extent to which the sample represents a heterogeneous population. For economy, however, one may choose to employ cluster sampling, a procedure in which groupings (clusters) of prospective respondents are randomly selected and then respondents are randomly selected from within the selected clusters. For example, a sample of university students could be selected by first obtaining a random sample of universities and then using SRS to select specific students from each selected university. In this case, the cluster is university. Variants of cluster sampling include multiple stages, such as selecting students within colleges within universities within countries.

## Non-probability sampling

Non-probability sampling procedures generally base selection on availability or convenience. The commonality is that they do not provide any means by which to make valid inferences from the selected sample because one cannot determine sampling error. For example, accidental sampling involves "selecting" whoever is willing to respond to one's survey, a procedure that led editors of the *Literary Digest* to predict that Alf Landon would win the US presidential election in 1936; Franklin D. Roosevelt obtained 63 per cent of the votes. Similarly, quota sampling, non-randomly choosing respondents on the basis of categorical membership, in the 1948 US presidential election led to the infamous DEWEY DEFEATS TRUMAN headline.

There are, however, research purposes for which non-probability sampling is appropriate. For example, Abdalla (1991) attempted to explore gender differences in uses of social support to relieve job stress in Kuwait. Because no previous research on this topic had been conducted in Arab cultures, Abdalla was more interested in whether any gender differences could be identified than in how such differences could be used to predict males' and females' reactions to job stress. Thus, a non-probability sample of middle-level managers in Kuwait was sufficient for the research goal. In general, non-probability samples are appropriate whenever one does not wish to generalize beyond the specific sample of respondents.

## NATURALISTIC OBSERVATION

Whereas survey methods involve an interaction between the researcher and the respondent, naturalistic observation involves methods designed to examine behaviour without actually being a part of it, to avoid as much as possible interfering with what is being observed. Naturalistic observation typically involves collecting data in order to form new hypotheses and is particularly suited to exploratory and descriptive research purposes (Butler, Rice, & Wagstaff, 1963).

### Intrusion

If one is to observe events as they unfold, one must avoid intrusion, defined as anything that lessens the participants' perception of an event as natural (Tunnell, 1977). Intrusion can involve any aspect of an event; the behaviours that comprise the event, the setting in which it takes place, and the treatment of the participant by the researcher. With respect to behaviours, the key element is the degree to which those being observed are aware that they are being observed. The degree of intrusion into the setting is determined by the extent to which the event takes place in an environment the participant believes is a research setting. Natural settings include those normally frequented for purposes other than participating in research. Intrusion with respect to treatment refers to the extent to which the event could have occurred without the researcher's presence or influence.

The naturalness of the events being studied is a continuum rather than a dichotomy. Participants' perceptions of naturalness can vary from one end of the continuum to the other. Also, the mixture of behaviour, setting, and treatment makes some events more or less natural than others. Natural behaviours do not always occur in natural settings; they can arise from intrusive treatments, or arise under unusual settings, and so forth. The key to determining the naturalness of an event is attempting to understand what is going on from the participant's point of view.

### Selecting events

When selecting events, one must first decide which events are of interest, and then decide how to sample the specific events. The first decision, of course, depends on the hypotheses to be examined. Weick (1968) has categorized events on the basis of behaviours in which researchers are most often interested: non-verbal, spatial, extra linguistic, and linguistic.

Non-verbal behaviours are body movements that convey information. They may include facial expressions, eye contact, hand movements, posture, and so on. Spatial behaviours involve maintaining or altering distances among people or between people and objects; again, such behaviours convey information or reactions to another's behaviour. Extralinguistic behaviours include rate, tone, volume, and other similar characteristics of speech. Finally, linguistic behaviours refer to the content of speech or written material.

Deciding which behaviours from among an entire behavioural sequence to observe involves the general principles of sampling described for survey methods above, but there are a few aspects specific to naturalistic observation. Generally, sampling events involves either time or event sampling. Time sampling, as the term implies, refers to selecting a specific interval of time during which observations will be made. One may sample continuously, that is observe the entire behavioural sequence, but such extensive selection clearly must be reserved for sequences of short duration. Alternatively, one may employ time-point sampling, in which one selects a specific time such as the top of every hour and observes whatever occurs at that moment, or employ time-interval sampling, in which one selects a specific interval such as the last five minutes of every hour and observes ongoing behaviours during the interval. Event sampling involves observing one behaviour contingent upon the presence of another behaviour and is usually used for hypotheses about relationships between two variables or when knowing the duration of the behaviour is not necessary. Event sampling provides only relative information; only continuous time sampling enables absolute measurements of the behaviour.

## Coding

Coding involves interpreting what has been recorded, and it is very often accomplished at the same time as recording. It may be used to represent behaviour. For example, Leventhal and Sharp (1965) developed an elaborate system of symbols used to record facial expressions, and LaFrance (1979) developed a similar system for arm positions. The symbols used are a shorthand for the actual behaviour, but they don't necessarily ascribe any meaning to the behaviour.

More often than not, however, coding involves both recording and interpreting an observation. The best known of such systems is the interaction process analysis (IPA) system developed by Bales (1970). IPA allows observers to record inferred meanings for linguistic, extralinguistic, and non-verbal behaviours among groups. The IPA is one of many examples of check-list coding schemes. Barker (1963) developed an elaborate check-list of social behaviours, while Benjamin's (1979) system deals with interpersonal motivations.

An alternative to check-list systems is the unstructured or ethological system, also known as natural history. The ethological system involves a detailed and comprehensive recording of behaviours with little or no inferred meaning. For example, McGrew (1972) used an ethological system to categorize 110 different behaviours of nursery schoolchildren's social interactions. Although use of an ethological system does not preclude the eventual interpretation of one's observations, it does preclude mixing recording with interpretation.

When the behaviour being observed is linguistic, content analysis is usually the coding mechanism (Holsti, 1968; Lasswell, Lerner, & Pool, 1952). One may use content analysis to establish authorship (Rokeach, Homant, & Penner, 1970), authors' attitudes (Seider, 1974), cultural beliefs (Zimbardo & Meadow, 1974), persuasion tactics (McHugh, Lanzetta, Sullivan, Masters, & Englis, 1985), social learning (Kounin & Gump, 1961), and social motivation (Runyan, 1982).

There are two major types of content that one may analyse – manifest and latent. Manifest content is the physical or non-inferential material that makes up a message, and is usually coded in terms of words or letters in written material, words and pauses in audio material, concrete actions in visual material, and so forth. It is relatively easy to code reliably; few people would disagree about the presence or absence of a word or an action in an observation. Latent content refers to inferred, underlying, or hidden meaning in material. It may be coded in terms of words or actions, and it usually involves inferences from sentences, paragraphs, facial expressions, and tone of voice, as well as other indications of meaning. Because coding latent content involves making inferences about the manifest content of an archive, latent content is generally less reliable than manifest content. On the other hand, latent content may be the only way to operationalize some concepts. Evaluative assertion analysis (Osgood, 1959) is frequently used for coding latent content.

When check-lists or rating scales are used to simultaneously record and code actions, at least some interpretation occurs before any observations are made. Choosing the categories to be included on the check-list, or choosing an existing check-list, involves interpreting what will and will not be important before any observation occurs. Gellert (1955) has noted that the number of different categories and the number of coding errors are directly related. Similarly, category abstractness and error are directly related: the more a coder/recorder must do in terms of interpretation, the more likely it is that he or she will make a mistake.

Dunnette (1966) described four sources of error that reduce reliability: inadequate sampling, chance response tendencies, changes in the participant, and changes in the situation. Inadequate sampling occurs when only a subset of events is recorded and the sampling process is not systematic. That is, errors occur when observers do not have or fail to follow a system for selecting observations. Chance response tendencies involve replacing formal category definitions with idiosyncratic definitions. Poorly trained or inadequately motivated observers are often the sources of such errors, but not the only sources. For example, chance response tendencies are more likely to occur when using abstract categories in a check-list system. Assessing inter-observer reliability enables one to estimate the extent of sampling and chance response errors. The latter types of errors are more difficult to detect, and may in fact not be considered errors at all. That is, changes in the individual(s) or situation(s) being observed may result from reactivity, or they may be part of the natural progression of the event. The use of unobtrusive measures (e.g. Webb, Campbell, Schwartz, & Sechrest, 1966) is the most effective way to avoid reactivity.

## CASE-STUDIES

Case-studies involve intensive research of a single individual or event. For the former, one can employ survey methods or naturalistic observation, adapted, of course, for the much smaller sample size. For the latter, one must employ participant observation, an observational method in which the researcher becomes part of the events being observed (Liebow, 1967). In participant observation, recording equipment includes little more than paper and pencil (and perhaps a word processor). The research tool of greatest importance is the field journal or notebook into which observations are entered.

### Sampling

Whereas naturalistic observation involves selecting behaviours, participant observation is more likely to involve selecting a setting in which to observe the event(s) of interest. Sampling in participant observation involves first selecting the group of people to be observed and then locating settings in which those people can be found. This can sometimes be accomplished via informants, who often provide the information necessary to employ one of three types of sampling suggested by McCall and Simmons (1969): quota, snowball, and deviant case.

Quota sampling, selecting sampling elements on the basis of categories assumed to exist within the population, involves purposefully searching out participants who fit the research requirements. Snowball sampling involves obtaining suggestions for other participants from those one has already observed. Also called key informant sampling, snowball sampling is analogous to a salesperson asking the most recent customer for names of prospective customers. Deviant case sampling involves observing individuals who do not seem to fit some pattern exhibited by others. Insights into reasons for engaging in an activity often can be discovered from those who choose not to engage in the activity.

## Hypothesis testing

Testing hypotheses in case-studies typically involves negative case analysis, which includes searching for data that disconfirm a tentative hypothesis, revising the hypothesis to include the disconfirming data, searching for more data, and so on. Whatever hypothesis survives this procedure is very likely to contain both necessary and sufficient causes. The depth with which one can test a hypothesis using negative case analysis often makes up for the fact that the results of case-studies can rarely be generalized beyond the individual(s) or event(s) studied.

## FURTHER READING

Dane, F. C. (1990). *Research methods*. Pacific Grove, CA: Brooks/Cole.

Fassnacht, G. (1982). *Theory and practice of observing behaviour* (trans. C. Bryant). London: Academic Press.

Fowler, F. J., Jr (1988). *Survey research methods*. Newbury Park, CA: Sage.

Miller, D. C. (1991). *Handbook of research design and social measurement*. Newbury Park, CA: Sage.

Yin, R. K. (1989). *Case study research: Design and methods*. Newbury Park, CA: Sage.

## REFERENCES

Abdalla, I. A. (1991). Social support and gender responses to job stress in an Arab culture. *Journal of Social Behavior and Personality, 6*(7), 273–288.

Ajzen, I., & Madden, T. J. (1986). Prediction of goal-directed behavior: Attitudes, intentions, and perceived behavioral control. *Journal of Experimental Social Psychology, 22*, 453–474.

Altman, I. (1975). *The environment and social behavior: Privacy, personal space, territory, and crowding*. Pacific Grove, CA: Brooks/Cole.

Bales, R. F. (1970). *Personality and interpersonal behavior*. New York: Holt, Rinehart & Winston.

Barker, R. G. (Ed.) (1963). *The stream of behavior*. New York: Appleton-Century-Crofts.

Benjamin, L. S. (1979). Use of structural analysis of social behavior (SASB) and Markov chains to study dyadic interactions. *Journal of Abnormal Psychology, 88*, 303–319.

Bishop, G. F., Oldendick, R. W., & Tuchfarber, A. J. (1983). Effects of filler questions in public opinion surveys. *Public Opinion Quarterly, 47*, 528–546.

Bradburn, N. M., & Sudman, S. (1979). *Improving interview method and questionnaire design*. San Francisco, CA: Jossey-Bass.

Butler, J. M., Rice, L. N., & Wagstaff, A. K. (1963). *Quantitative naturalistic research*. Englewood Cliffs, NJ: Prentice-Hall.

Cannell, C. F., Miller, P. V., & Oksenberg, L. (1981). Research on interviewing techniques. In S. Leinhardt (Ed.) *Sociological methodology* (pp. 389–437). San Francisco, CA: Jossey-Bass.

Dillman, D. A. (1978). *Mail and telephone surveys: The total design method.* New York: Wiley.

Dunnette, M. D. (1966). *Personnel selection and placement.* Belmont, CA: Wadsworth.

Fazio, R. H., & Zanna, M. P. (1981). Direct experience and attitude-behavior consistency. *Advances in Experimental Social Psychology, 14,* 161–202.

Fazio, R. H., Lenn, T. M., & Effrein, E. A. (1983/1984). Spontaneous attitude formation. *Social Cognition, 2,* 217–234.

Feldman, R. M. (1990). Settlement-identity: Psychological bonds with home place in a mobile society. *Environment and Behaviour, 22*(2), 183–229.

Fiske, S. T., & Taylor, S. E. (1991). *Social cognition* (2nd edn). New York: McGraw-Hill.

Gellert, E. (1955). Systematic observation: A method in child study. *Harvard Educational Review, 25,* 179–195.

Groves, R. M., & Kahn, R. L. (1979). *Surveys by telephone: A national comparison with personal interviews.* New York: Academic Press.

Holsti, O. R. (1968). Content analysis. In G. Lindzey & E. Aronson (Eds) *The handbook of social psychology* (pp. 596–692). Menlo Park, CA: Addison-Wesley.

Jourard, S. M. (1971). *Self-disclosure.* New York: Wiley.

Kallgren, C. A., & Wood, W. (1986). Access to attitude-relevant information in memory as a determinant of attitude-behavior consistency. *Journal of Experimental Social Psychology, 22,* 328–338.

Kalton, G., Roberts, J., & Holt, D. (1980). The effects of offering a middle response option with opinion questions. *Statistician, 29,* 11–24.

Kish, L. (1965). *Survey sampling.* New York: Wiley.

Kounin, J., & Gump, P. (1961). The comparative influence of punitive and non-punitive teachers upon children's concepts of school misconduct. *Journal of Educational Psychology, 52,* 44–49.

LaFrance, M. (1979). Nonverbal synchrony and rapport: Analysis by the cross-lagged panel technique. *Social Psychology Quarterly, 42,* 66–70.

Lasswell, H. D., Lerner, D., & Pool, I. de S. (1952). *The comparative study of symbols.* Stanford, CA: Stanford University Press.

Leventhal, H., & Sharp, E. (1965). Facial expressions as indicators of distress. In S. Thompkins & C. Izard (Eds) *Affect, cognition, and personality* (pp. 296–318). New York: Springer.

Liebow, E. (1967). *Tally's corner.* Boston, MA: Little, Brown.

*Literary Digest* (1936). Landon, 1,293,669: Roosevelt, 972,897. *Literary Digest,* 31 October, pp. 5–6.

McCall, G. C., & Simmons, J. L. (Eds) (1969). *Issues in participant observation.* Reading, MA: Addison-Wesley.

McGrew, W. C. (1972). *An ethological study of children's behavior.* New York: Academic Press.

McHugo, G. J., Lanzetta, J. T., Sullivan, D. G., Masters, R. D., & Englis, B. G. (1985). Emotional reactivity to a political leader's expressive displays. *Journal of Personality and Social Psychology, 49,* 1513–1529.

Metts, S. (1989). An exploratory investigation of deception in close relationships. *Journal of Social and Personal Relationships, 6,* 159–179.

Osgood, C. E. (1959). The representational model and relevant research methods. In I. de S. Pool (Ed.) *Trends in content analysis* (pp. 33–88). Urbana, IL: University of Illinois Press.

Rokeach, M., Homant, R., & Penner, L. (1970). A value analysis of the disputed federalist papers. *Journal of Personality and Social Psychology*, *16*, 245–250.

Ross, L., Greene, D., & House, P. (1977). The "false consensus effect": An egocentric bias in social perception and attribution processes. *Journal of Experimental Social Psychology*, *13*, 279–301.

Runyan, W. M. (1982). *Life histories and psychobiography: Explorations in theory and method*. New York: Oxford University Press.

Schuman, H., & Kalton, G. (1985) Survey methods. In G. Lindzey & E. Aronson (Eds) *Handbook of social psychology* (3rd edn, vol. 1, pp. 635–697). Reading, MA: Addison-Wesley.

Schwartz, S. H. (1978). Temporal instability as a moderator of the attitude–behavior relationship. *Journal of Personality and Social Psychology*, *36*, 715–724.

Seider, M. S. (1974). American big business ideology: A content analysis of executive speeches. *American Sociological Review*, *39*, 802–815.

Skogan, W. G. (1981). *Issues in the measurement of victimization*. Washington, DC: Bureau of Justice Statistics, US Department of Justice (NCJ-74682).

Tunnell, G. B. (1977). Three dimensions of naturalness: An expanded definition of field research. *Psychological Bulletin*, *84*, 426–437.

Turner, A. G. (1972). *The San Jose methods test of known crime victims*. Washington, DC: National Criminal Justice Information and Statistics Service, US Department of Justice.

Tversky, A., & Kahneman, D. (1974). Judgment under uncertainty: Heuristics and biases. *Science*, *815*, 1124–1131.

Tversky, A., & Kahneman, D. (1980). Causal schemes in judgments under uncertainty. In M. Fishbein (Ed.) *Progress in social psychology* (vol. 1, pp. 49–72) Hillsdale, NJ: Lawrence Erlbaum.

Van Drusen, R. A., & Zill, N. (Eds) (1975). *Basic background items for U.S. household surveys*. Washington, DC: Center for Coordination of Research on Social Indicators, Social Science Research Council.

Weaver, C. N., & Swanson, C. L. (1974). Validity of reported date of birth, salary, and seniority. *Public Opinion Quarterly*, *38*, 69–80.

Webb, E. J., Campbell, D. T., Schwartz, R. D., & Sechrest, L. (1966). *Unobtrusive measures*. Chicago, IL: Rand McNally.

Weick, K. E. (1968). Systematic observational methods. In G. Lindzey & E. Aronson (Eds) *The handbook of social psychology* (Vol. 2, pp. 370–404). Reading, MA: Addison-Wesley.

Zimbardo, P. G., & Meadow, W. (1974). *Sexism springs eternal in the* Reader's Digest. Presented at Western Psychological Association, San Francisco, CA, April.

# 6

# ETHICAL ISSUES IN PSYCHOLOGICAL RESEARCH

## Anthony Gale
### University of Southampton, England

Moral discourse is like the food industry – it is hard to imagine a time when it will be short of business. Moral debate is an essential element in human existence, and ethics has been a central issue in philosophy for centuries. We have a preoccupation with our duties and responsibilities to others, our notions of what is right and wrong, and our positive or negative evaluations of the actions of both ourselves and others. Hardly a day can pass when we do not make a moral judgement about the conduct of others. Philosophers have tried to identify the ethical bases for our relationships with other human beings (for example, why it is wrong to lie, to steal, or to murder), or with society at large (for example, why altruism is better than selfishness, whether we have a moral duty to the poor or to the state). But you will be disappointed if you take a course in ethics in the hope of getting straightforward moral answers about how you should lead your life. As Sartre said, we are condemned to be free.

## MORALS, ETHICS, SOCIAL NORMS, AND THE PSYCHOLOGIST

### Moral debate is hard work

The outsider to ethical debate finds it hard to appreciate that basic ethical propositions are not reducible to other propositions, such as psychological propositions – for example, that the good is that which makes people happy. Formal ethical debate calls for coherent logical argument among people who typically share basic ethical beliefs but differ as to how such fundamental principles may be applied in a particular case. Moral decisions are almost always a compromise, balancing the imperatives of one principle against the imperatives of another and taking into account the particular circumstances. There are no simple answers. Unfortunately, however, few of us are accustomed to sustained ethical debate. Rollin (1985) suggests that much of the debate about the moral status of research animals in psychology is irrational because

> most people's moral ideas are acquired piecemeal from a variety of sources throughout life, such as parents, teachers, friends, education, reading and films; there is little guarantee that these ideas will form a coherent whole. In fact, most people are not even consciously aware of their moral assumptions. (p. 921)

An informal survey of my academic colleagues shows that few of them remember being taught about ethics during their psychological education. There is little evidence that formal experience of ethical debate is considered an important element in the psychological curriculum (Gale, 1990).

One aspect of ethical conduct in science is taught to students implicitly by a sort of osmosis, and that is the principle that psychology shares with other sciences, for integrity and honesty in the reporting of data. It is not clear how students learn to be honest in their research endeavours, and there are notorious examples of alleged cheating and selectivity in psychological research. For example, Hearnshaw (1979) concluded in his biography of Burt that this distinguished and respected psychologist had for some years been guilty of scientific malpractice, although such conclusions are not shared by others (see Fletcher, 1991; Joynson, 1989).

## Ethical debate in psychology is not straightforward

Given that the psychological sciences are concerned with the study of people, the discipline has a special set of moral concerns that do not apply in other sciences. The problem of ethics in psychological research is daunting and *any* psychological research project calls for non-trivial ethical debate. While learned and professional societies such as the American Psychological Association (APA) and the British Psychological Society (BPS) publish ethical guidelines for the conduct of research, such guidelines prove difficult to apply in any hard-and-fast way, in any particular research context, and they remain merely as guidelines. They continue to be criticized on grounds of vagueness (Aitkenhead & Dordoy, 1983) and the majority of scientific journals *assume* that ethical concerns have been considered by the researcher, rather than requiring a formal statement to that effect.

Schlenker and Forsyth (1977) warn psychologists to be aware of the consequences for psychology of different philosophical approaches to ethical principles, which they identify as: *teleological*, where the morality of an action is ultimately judged by its consequences; the *deontological* approach, which rejects consequences as a basis for judgement and appeals to fundamental principles or categorical absolutes derived from natural law; and *skepticism*, which assumes that inviolate moral codes can never be formulated, and includes approaches such as cultural relativism, ethical egoism, and emotivism. They showed experimentally that individuals' moral positions (which of the three approaches they accept) affect their evaluation of the ethicality of particular research studies. Psychological moral discourse is not different from general moral discourse; it will always be hard for participants to agree.

## Psychological ethics must keep pace with social change

It is an interesting fact that the APA and BPS codes or guidelines are reviewed periodically; both societies published revised codes in 1990, showing that some aspects at least cannot depend on absolutes or universal truths. One reason for the need to update the codes is the changing context of psychological research and the possibility that new research issues (for example, sexual behaviour in the context of AIDS) might highlight new ethical problems (Melton & Gray, 1988). A more potent reason is the changing views of society at large about the nature of individual rights and the extent to which psychological research is seen to be insensitive to or to invade such rights; thus, for example, the changing approach to adolescent offenders, as people who should be consulted about their treatment rather than as people upon whom decisions should be imposed by experts, has created new restrictions on research into corrective intervention (Mulvey & Phelps, 1988).

Psychology itself might contribute to changing views of the individual. For example, humanistic psychology has had an impact on notions of personal autonomy and freedom of choice and was a reaction to more psychoanalytic-deterministic or behaviourist constructions of the person. More recently, feminist psychology has increased public awareness of institutionalized oppression of women; both the APA and the BPS, in internal documentation and in their scientific journals, prohibit the use of gender-related language, but many further issues remain to be resolved (Denmark, Russo, Frieze, & Sechzer, 1988; see also Condor, 1991, discussed below).

Thus new research, changing views of the person, and the influence of new insights in psychology itself, demonstrate the changing sociocultural background against which ethical codes need to be deployed or are seen to be adequate or salient. New legal rulings might actually restrict psychological research or prove so threatening that research might not be done for fear that the researcher becomes exposed to potential legal action. Appelbaum and Rosenbaum (1989) discuss the implications of the California Supreme Court ruling in the Tarasoff case. Ms Tarasoff was a student; another student informed his therapist at the university counselling centre that he intended to kill her; the therapist informed the police and the second student was detained; but, when the police released him, believing he was not a threat, the counsellors took no further action to warn others or to ensure that he returned to treatment; he then killed Ms Tarasoff. The Supreme Court held the university responsible on the ground that the counsellors were analogous to medical staff who can know the dangers to others of a patient's infectious illness or who negligently allow a violent patient to escape from custody; thus they had a special relationship with the murderer and "a duty to protect" others from his violence. Appelbaum and Rosenbaum (1989) consider analogous research circumstances in which a researcher might be said to have such a duty and conclude that the relationship would need to be analogous to a clinical relationship. Otherwise, they suggest that psychological research on child abuse, violence, substance abuse, and AIDS might be compromised. Similarly, Mulvey and Phelps (1988) appeal for special protection for the privacy of participants in AIDS research, where the researcher might feel pressurized to report to the authorities respondents' confessions to failing to declare their infection when having sexual intercourse.

An interesting feature of current ethical guidelines and psychological research reports is that the term "subjects" has begun, since the early 1980s, be replaced by the term "participants", and this also reflects a changing view of the individual in psychology itself. There has been a historical shift in the perception of the role of the participant in the laboratory from object to person (Silverman, 1977). As Schultz (1969) put it, the I–It relationship has been replaced by the I–You relationship, which in turn has implications for the sorts of procedures that psychological researchers will deploy in the laboratory.

## The dilemma: benefits versus costs

Two implicit fundamental ethical beliefs in psychology are first, that the pursuit of psychological knowledge is inherently good, not least because increased understanding could enhance the human condition, and second, that in psychological research participants should be protected from stress, undue invasions of privacy, and other forms of exploitation. These two commitments (to increase knowledge and to protect the individual) can come into direct conflict when the needs of the research seem potentially to undermine the integrity or status of the participant, and that is the central dilemma.

Neff, Iwata, and Page (1986), in a historical review, cite several dramatic examples of medical and psychological/behavioural research which involved the abuse of participants and which caused a public furore: in a stress experiment, participants were led to believe that they were in danger of losing their lives through a simulated plane malfunction; the injection of live cancer cells into chronically ill patients to study the development of antibodies without informing them; the recording of juror behaviour, without their knowledge, with concealed microphones; withholding treatment from 400 subjects in a 40-year study of the long-term effects of syphilis. They might also have included the work of Zimbardo (1973) in which students took the roles of warders and prisoners in a simulated prison, and the researchers had to stop the study early because of the undesirable compliant and punitive behaviours exhibited by participants.

Ask any psychology student about ethics in psychological research and the immediate answer will refer to Milgram's (1963) study of obedience. Milgram believed that context, and in particular obedience to authority, could influence otherwise ordinary and decent folk to act in violent and oppressive ways to others. He thought it was naïve to believe that only certain sorts of people could be guilty of aggression. The abstract of his 1963 paper provides the essential outline of the study:

> This article describes a procedure for the study of destructive obedience in the laboratory. It consists of ordering a naïve S to administer increasingly more severe punishment to a victim in the context of a learning experiment. Punishment is administered by means of a shock generator with 30 gradual switches ranging from Slight Shock to Danger: Severe Shock. The victim is a confederate of the E. The primary dependent variable is the maximum shock the S is willing to administer before he refuses to continue further. 26 Ss obeyed the experimental commands fully, and administered the highest shock on the generator. 14 Ss broke off the experiment at some point after the victim protested and refused to provide further answers. The procedure created extreme levels of nervous tension in some Ss.

Profuse sweating, trembling, and stuttering were typical expressions of this emotional disturbance. One unexpected sign of tension – yet to be explained – was the regular occurrence of nervous laughter, which in some Ss developed into uncontrollable seizures. The variety of interesting behavioral dynamics observed in the experiment, the reality of the situation for the S, and the possibility of parametric variation within the framework of the procedure, point to the fruitfulness of further study. (Milgram, 1963, p. 371)

To the modern critic, the formal technical and matter-of-fact description of the work, the detached clinical description of participants' reactions, and the exhortation to use the technique for further parametric research, add to the sense of horror. Publication of the research brought vilification from other psychologists and from the press; Milgram's study has become a notorious illustration of the alleged wickedness of psychological researchers. Although it occurred many years ago, it is still cited in introductory texts as a key study.

Among the criticisms of Milgram were: making people do things in the laboratory that they would never do in real life, lowering participants' self-esteem by showing them what evil they were capable of, causing long-term harm to their perception of themselves, causing extreme emotional reactions, causing reactions that neither he nor the participants could explain (the laughter), deceiving participants (because no shock was delivered, the apparent recipient of shock was a confederate, and his screams of pain were enacted), instructing people to harm other people, creating experimental conditions under which participants were obliged to follow instructions and found it difficult to withdraw, damaging the reputation of psychology by making it hard for others to conduct research, damaging psychological research by making participants suspicious of being misled, and demonstrating to totalitarian regimes how easy it would be to carry out torture (Baumrind, 1964; Kelman, 1967).

It seems that Milgram was possibly harmed more than were his participants, only 1 per cent of whom said a year later in a follow-up survey that they regretted participating, the majority expressing a positive view of their participation (Milgram, 1977). One participant wrote to Milgram thanking him for making him aware of what he was capable of and the need to resist unacceptable instructions from people in authority. But the harm to psychology itself is hard to calculate.

To illustrate the ethical complexity of the issue and the fact that condemnation of Milgram, while understandable, is not the only possible reaction, let us look further at the positive side of the equation. Did Milgram also instruct us in some important moral lessons, for which some sort of price might be worth paying?

Milgram changed our view of obedience, showing that the majority of us might be capable in appropriate circumstances of committing atrocities, an important if distasteful insight into the human condition. Thus, under appropriate conditions, concentration camps could appear in several cultures

97

or political regimes. Such a revelation could affect not only our explanations for and treatment of those who commit acts of violence but our views of major conflict, undermining xenophobic bigotry, teaching us humility about what could happen in our own society, and enhancing inter alia international understanding, and promoting forgiveness for past wrongs.

It might also serve to explain the fascination people appear to have with human tragedies and disasters as portrayed in the media, and the ready moral condemnation we indulge in when the antisocial actions of others are in the spotlight. In psychoanalytic terms, both contexts enable us to operate ego-defences in socially acceptable ways, revealing to the astute observer both our potential for violence and its social suppression from early childhood. An important lesson for the psychologist is that explanations couched in personal terms (such as "the authoritarian personality") serve to minimize our appreciation of the role that politics, power, and the prevailing ideology may have on individual actions.

### The potential for disrepute: can psychology ever win?

The key ethical question raised by Milgram's research is whether the benefits of such revelations justify the steps taken to achieve them. In several areas of psychology it is clear that the results of psychological research could be turned to good or ill; conditioning principles, which have helped so admirably in the rehabilitation of long-term psychiatric patients, might also be deployed in the humiliation and torturing of political prisoners, for which there is a ready audience, as the work of Amnesty International so frequently testifies. Theories and research on attitude change could be used not only in health education (for smoking cessation programmes, say) but also for the promotion of political extremism (such as the acceptance of "ethnic cleansing" in the Balkans). Defendants of research on gender differences and ethnic differences in cognitive processes have had to fight hard to sustain the view that such research is actually potentially beneficial for under-represented minority groups (Scarr, 1988) and need not be merely treated as fuel for right-wing extremists. How easy is it, though, to predict in advance, what use (good or ill?) will be made of your research findings? Einstein is alleged to have said that had he known, he would have become a watchmaker.

### Principles governing the scientist–participant relationship

Milgram's studies highlight some of the key issues in psychological research: deception, voluntary consent, subject discomfort, and freedom to withdraw. Other issues that have attracted attention are the role of post-experimental debriefing, and breaches of privacy and of confidentiality. Research does not have to be dramatic nor have the potential notoriety of the original Milgram study to create such concerns. In every research study a calculation needs to be made in advance of the cost–benefit equation.

The social psychology of the psychology experiment reveals an asymmetrical power relationship between experimenter and participant, and the rules and roles of the situation give the experimenter considerable authority. Power is also associated with responsibility. An important issue, even in mundane and apparently non-controversial research, is whether the actions of psychologists in research settings are in any way at variance with what are considered to be the socially or culturally acceptable ways of treating others in everyday social intercourse or in analogous situations of unequal status, such as the classroom or the doctor's surgery (Gale & Chapman, 1984).

### Barriers to open debate

Many of the ethical issues surrounding psychological research are too hot to handle. That may be the reason why explicit discussion of ethics is so rarely an essential ingredient of undergraduate curricula. In the past, for example, many undergraduate students were required to participate in research as part of their psychological training, so much so that 80 per cent of the psychological research from 1950 to the mid-1970s could be described as "the psychology of the sophomore" (Silverman, 1977). Clearly, such participation could be beneficial for them, increasing their understanding of psychological science. But such a requirement also creates an opportunity for exploitation, since students might wish to comply with the wishes of their teachers or even fear lower grades as a reprisal if they refuse to participate. Explicit class discussion of the need for voluntary consent might make such students resentful of the requirement to participate. Thus there is an incentive for full discussion of ethical concerns in research to remain on a hidden agenda.

### Psychologists are only human

Academic psychologists make a living out of psychological research, and their career, salary, self-esteem, and peer recognition are all based on research achievement. Any prescription that seeks to restrict their freedom also restricts their career prospects. Some commentators have coyly asked why there is relatively little empirical research into the ethics of research (Aitkenhead & Dordoy, 1983), the implication being that failure to address such important issues is a defence mechanism in the form of denial. Psychologists, like everyone else, are subject to value judgements of which they are not necessarily aware and to a tendency to bias judgements to their own benefit; thus persistence in behaviour that is self-serving, without conscious debate on its moral implications, is to be expected.

## The danger of public condemnation

As the findings of psychology penetrate public consciousness there is an increasing likelihood that such findings will influence public policy; but public policy is itself influenced by political pressures and beliefs, so that psychological findings in such spheres are always likely to provoke negative public reaction on the part of vested interests. For example, any research into the impact of day-care on young children is likely to offend some interest group: those who defend women's right to work will reject evidence of negative effects, those who defend "traditional family values" will reject evidence of positive effects.

The image of psychological science as value-free has become harder to sustain. Starr (1988), accusing others of moral cowardice, declared that she was prepared to go into exile, in the eventuality of negative public condemnation, if the results of her work on multracial fostering proved to be politically unacceptable. She wanted to know whether ethnic minority children raised in white middle-class homes would show major intellectual gains.

## The development of formal guidelines for the conduct of research

Where there is the potential for exploitation and public acrimony it is essential to have formal codes of conduct, both to protect the individual participant and to offer professional protection to the researcher. The history of the evolution of the APA code for research illustrates the effort, dedication, and resources devoted to the development of the code, which had first appeared in 1953. Between 1966 and 1972, when the full ethical code was finally published, the following steps were taken: literature review, pilot questionnaire to 1,000 members, full questionnaire to 9,000 members, soliciting of 2,000 ethical problems from a broad range of researchers, revision of draft principles, further questionnaires to a second sample of 9,000 members and selected groups, soliciting of 3,000 further descriptions of research problems, interviews with 35 experts (journal editors, research directors, experts on ethics, on hypnosis, and so on), discussion of the draft principles at several scientific meetings, consultation with 800 academic institutions requesting full debate and discussion, consultations with members of other disciplines (philosophers, anthropologists, lawyers, and others), publication of the revised version in 1972 including a requirement for five-yearly reviews, which led to revised publication in 1981 and 1990 (American Psychological Association, 1982, 1990). The BPS code also underwent major revisions published in 1978 and 1990 but deploying a much more modest methodology (British Psychological Society, 1991).

## Do values differ on the two sides of the Atlantic?

It is clear that both learned societies (which are the largest psychological societies in the world) demonstrated a strong sense of social responsibility and sensitivity in developing their codes, although the element of self-protection is also hard to deny. It is evident, for example, that the APA code is more explicit and more comprehensive than the BPS code (for example, on matters of competence, protection of minority groups, teachers' responsibilities, sensitivity to the influence of personal values, and in the combination of professional practice and research codes and human and animal research within one document).

## A brief comment on research with other species

This chapter does not include a detailed debate on the important moral controversy surrounding the use of non-human species in psychological research; the reader may wish to refer to American Psychological Association (1990), Bateson (1986), British Psychological Society (1991), Experimental Psychology Society (1986), Gray (1987), and Miller (1985). Wadeley (1991) lists five key guidelines for animal research in psychology:

1 full knowledge of the law governing animal experimentation
2 thoroughgoing knowledge of the reactions of different species, in the interests of reducing distress
3 humane practices in the breeding, capture, and transport of animals and the use of the smallest samples feasible
4 minimization of pain and distress
5 use of invasive procedures only by competent and fully licensed individuals.

Herzog (1988), in an amusing but challenging article on the moral status of mice, asserts that it rests on the values of humans and the roles humans require mice to play and not in the intrinsic qualities of the mouse. Thus on or within reach of one campus there were four categories of mouse: the *good* mice (used in experiments and protected by legal/ethical codes and veterinary care), the *bad* mice (free-ranging, disease-transmitting pests which suffer painful deaths through traps), *feeder* (morally neutral?) mice used to feed other species, like snakes, required in research, and his son's pet mouse, whose death led to a funeral and tombstone:

> The moral judgements we make about other species are neither logical nor consistent. Rather, they are the result of both cerebral and visceral components of the human mind . . . the roles that animals play in our lives and the labels we attach to them, deeply influence our sense of what is ethical. (Herzog, 1988, p. 474).

Rollin (1985) suggests two principles that should guide decisions to use animals in research: first, the utilitarian principle, by which the potential benefit (to humans or animals) clearly outweighs the pain and suffering to be experienced, and second, the rights principle, whereby the conduct of the research maximizes the animal's potential for living its life according to its nature. Rollin suggests that as a first step we should make the assumption that animals have the same rights as humans, or at least we should use the human case as an analog. That is a most humane principle; unfortunately, our discussion will reveal that consideration of the rights of human participants in psychological research is not straightforward by any means.

## ETHICAL GUIDELINES FOR THE CONDUCT OF RESEARCH

### An obligation for all psychological researchers

Individuals wishing to conduct psychological research, whether they be fully fledged psychologists, students, or members of another profession, are strongly advised to study both the APA and BPS Principles. The codes reflect careful, humane, and considered attempts to guide the nature of psychological research in the interests of participants. Nevertheless, the codes continue to be criticized for perceived shortcomings (Condor, 1991, see below).

The dangers to the discipline of psychology of failing to enforce such codes are legion. For example, in the United Kingdom, there are upwards of 20,000 18-year-old school students taking the Advanced Level examination in psychology, which typically requires students to conduct five research studies. Many of the teachers are not qualified psychologists; there are thus 100,000 opportunities each year for examples of abuse of participants and for public scandal, easily fed by the prurience of the mass media.

Table 1 provides a schematic version of the key features of a combination of the APA and BPS Principles. The distillation focuses on the aspects of the codes particularly related to research; the APA code refers also to guidelines for professional conduct in the practice of applied psychology, which the BPS deals with in separate documents.

## LOOKING CLOSE AT THE PRINCIPLES: CONCEPTUAL ISSUES AND RESEARCH FINDINGS

We shall now examine the central issues of deception and consent and argue that there are dangers of intellectual and practical lip-service to the principles if researchers do not consider the psychological limits to consent and the research that has been conducted about consent itself. In other words, the publication of the Principles and psychologists' acceptance of them should not lead us to a false sense of security, nor indeed to overestimate participants' negative reactions to research procedures. Moreover, the terms used in the Principles are everyday or vernacular terms, lacking legal or technical precision.

*Table 1* A distillation of the American Psychological Association and British Psychological Society ethical principles for the conduct of research with human participants

*Responsibility*
Psychologists are responsible for their research; plan it considering the ethical implications for those involved, conducting a cost–benefit analysis, bearing in mind both the potential gains to psychological science and human welfare, and the risks to participants; appreciate that they might need the advice of others to fully understand its potential impact on particular groups; report it accurately, and are honest about its interpretation, do not suppress disconfirming data, recognizing inter alia that it might be construed to the detriment of others; avoid conflicts of interest which may limit their objectivity; do not lay claim to work that is not their own and acknowledge the contributions of others; prevent distortion of their findings by others; are sensitive to community values; offer a model to students of integrity and objective scholarship; ensure that those conducting research on their behalf share the full sense of ethical responsibility; are aware of political or other pressures that might lead to the misuse of psychological knowledge; treat research participants with respect, avoiding all exploitation, such as sexual harassment; take personal responsibility to correct any harm that occurs to participants as a result of the research; and, where colleagues persist in unprofessional conduct, seek to remonstrate with them and then, if necessary, take formal action against them by reporting them to their professional body.

*Competence*
To maintain high standards of competence, one has to keep up-to-date with scientific developments in one's field, obtain necessary training where necessary, not claim competence in techniques where one is not qualified, recognize the boundaries of one's expertise, appreciate that one's personal problems might influence professional judgement, and seek the advice of others where appropriate.

*Confidentiality*
Subject to any overriding legislation, psychologists respect all personal data about participants unless otherwise agreed in advance; resist improper pressures to release such information; conceal the identity of individuals in publishing data or in public lectures; ensure that all stored data are secure; inform participants if the data are to be shared with other researchers; have particular concern for the need to protect the interests of minors or others unable to give voluntary consent; do not reveal personal information to those who might misinterpret it.

*Consent*
Any feature of a study that might affect participants' willingness to take part should be disclosed in advance; where participants (such as young children or people with intellectual handicaps) might have limited understanding, attempts should be made to obtain real consent, apart from gaining consent from those *in loco parentis* or those with familial or other close links; where persons are detained, limits on true voluntary consent should be recognized; positions of authority over participants should not be used to pressurize them to participate; inducements should not be offered where risk is likely; withdrawal should be allowed at any time and the right to withdraw be made clear from the outset; participants should be free to insist that their data not be used and that records relating to them be destroyed; all promises given when securing consent must be fulfilled; in observational or covert research, where gaining consent

103

*Table 1* (*Continued*)

is not practicable, due regard should be given to cultural values and people's expectations relating to privacy in public places.

### Deception
In many cases, to reveal the full purposes of the study in advance might damage the research; under such circumstances the investigator has a responsibility to assess the scientific benefits, examine fully alternative procedures, consider the possible impact on participants, and ensure they are informed of the true nature of the study at the earliest possible stage; while debriefing after the study is completed is desirable in all cases, it should not be considered as a justification for unethical deception.

### Protection of participants
There is a primary responsibility for reducing risk, including identification of factors (such as medical history) that might compound risk; any undesirable consequences should be removed and participants should know that they can contact the investigator if any subsequent discomfort is experienced; care should be taken in discussing children with their parents, because information might be misinterpreted or given undue weight; participants should be informed of any psychological or physical problems that might come to light during the investigation, but bearing in mind the limits to the investigator's own competence.

## The psychology of consent

What does consent mean? It must assume three elements: knowledge and understanding of what is involved, competence, and voluntary choice. As Gale and Chapman (1984) point out, the investigator can explain a procedure in detail, but a participant will not have full knowledge of it until she or he has *experienced* it. Indeed, there is no guarantee that the investigators fully appreciate the procedure without undergoing the experience themselves. Given the necessary practice of deception in so much psychological research, it is hard to argue that full prior knowledge is guaranteed. And how much information should be given? Is the participant to receive a mini-lecture on previous research and the statistical robustness of research findings?

Again, the lack of competence of individuals may be the very reason why they are the subject of research (in research with young children, elderly people, infirm or handicapped people, or those in deep emotional distress). In the case of elderly people, some psychologists have too often assumed incompetence (Whitbourne & Hulicka, 1990) and thus sought the permission of others (say, superintendents of rest-homes) too readily.

Without considering the philosophical complexities of the notion of free will, we can appreciate what limits might be operating on voluntary choice: the status of the experimenter, our desire to please others, the desire not to let others down, the desire not to look foolish by insisting on withdrawing when an experiment is already underway. In other words, the social psychology of interpersonal relationships, and the behavioural notion that our actions are controlled by external reinforcement, argue against the truly voluntary action, in its vernacular sense, and apparently assumed in the Principles.

Neef et al. (1986), adopting a behavioural approach, suggest that psychological criteria for operationalizing consent can be devised, including formal tests of the would-be participants' ability to provide accurate descriptions of the experiment and what is involved, if necessary engaging in an iterative procedure until a criterion is reached.

Gale and Vetere (1987), in a critical ethical examination of their own research, confess that in their participant observation studies in family homes they sought the permission of parents (rather than children), did not appreciate the need to inform families of the full implications of publication, found it hard to disguise the identity of families in reports, changed their role inadvertently during the research from scientist to counsellor, and thus, in several ways, breached the full notion of voluntary consent. But the problems they encountered seem insoluble.

Several studies have explored participants' notions of consent, perceptions of deception, and what is acceptable in research, as a research enterprise in itself. For example Gerdes (1979) asked 655 college students of both genders for their reactions to 15 experiments involving various degrees of deception in which they had participated. She received an overwhelmingly positive reaction: respondents did not mind being deceived or having information withheld, and were willing to have a friend participate. In a study involving a factorial design in which stress, degree of deception, considerateness of experimenter, and degree of participation by the participant (active participation versus active role-play) were manipulated, Aitkenhead and Dordoy (1985) again showed that participants' reactions were predominantly positive. Michaels and Oetting (1979) gave participants two check-lists, one relating to personal and social benefits of research, and another specifying a range of stressful manipulations. They showed that their participants did not conduct a cost–benefit analysis; potential benefit did not influence their willingness to participate in a study, rather their primary concern was how much stress they might undergo. Finally, a study of cost–benefit analysis of students by Skinner, Berry, Biro, and Jackson (1991) showed that when the participants' view of the cost–benefit ratio is considered (rather than that of the researcher) subjects do conduct a cost–benefit analysis and are generally more willing to participate than the investigator's cost–benefit analysis predicts.

Studies such as these, stripping aside the possibility of participants' desire to give socially desirable responses (to please the investigator) seem to indicate that student populations are less concerned about the ethicality of some aspects of psychological research than are psychologists or learned societies. However, consideration of the distinctions drawn by Schlenker and Forsyth (1977) above will lead the reader to appreciate that for the deontological view, students' willingness to participate is irrelevant, since certain studies by virtue of their very nature will be seen to breach morality; for example, Baumrind (1971) in her critique of Milgram states: "Fundamental moral principles of reciprocity and justice are violated, when the research psychologist, using his position of trust, acts to deceive or degrade" (p. 890). Even broader moral issues might need to be considered in evaluating psychological research.

## WIDER ISSUES: THE MORAL STATUS OF PSYCHOLOGY WITHIN SOCIETY

### Special implications of socially sensitive research

Sieber and Stanley (1988) claim that some researchers have avoided conducting socially sensitive research through fear of the possible personal consequences, and they offer a taxonomy to guide the development of research proposals. They cite the study of Ceci, Peters, and Plotkin (1985), which showed that ethical review committees were twice as likely to reject hypothetical research proposals when they were socially sensitive (discrimination in job appointments) and that the grounds for rejection were largely in terms of potential political impact independent of the presence of ethical problems, such as deception. Sieber and Stanley (1988) list four stages of the research process at which ethical concerns arise: (1) formulation of the research question, (2) conduct of the research, (3) the research setting, and (4) the interpretation and application of findings.

The mere formulation of a research proposal, such as the measurement of ethnic differences in IQ or the genetic origins of violent dispositions can, they claim, raise ethical issues, even though the work is never carried out. Sieber and Stanley (1988) cite the impact of Freud's notion of women's sexual fantasies, anatomical inadequacy, and consequential penis envy (see Brennan, 1992), as still influencing social attitudes and social policy in spite of a 50-year lack of evidence to support the theory. Only public concern about the realities of child abuse has served to undermine the pervasiveness of Freud's views. Again, Sieber and Stanley (1988) point to the misleading ideas of Margaret Mead (1928, 1935, 1949) based on questionable methodology, as the source of the United States' sexual revolution. The failure, in the cultural revolution that her ideas promoted, to set limits on children's behaviour has, they claim, damaged a generation. Mead's notions of children's inherent goodness, combined with American optimism, served to promote and sustain particular views of child-rearing.

During the course of research, participants need to be protected, and the primary concern of ethical codes (as revealed in Table 1) is to focus on issues such as confidentiality, protection from harm, privacy, and deception. But as we saw earlier, information revealed by participants (say, concerning drugs, child abuse, intention to commit crime, or sexual behaviour in the context of AIDS) can create conflict between individual protection and the protection of society at large. In spite of a confidentiality undertaking, should a researcher seek to inform the sexual partner of an AIDS-carrying respondent? One consequence of such breaches of confidentiality could be the withdrawal of consent by particular groups and the undermining of future research, demonstrating yet again how one ethical principle fights against another.

In relation to institutional settings, Sieber and Stanley (1988) make the point that the organizational structure and atmosphere of the context of the research can have an impact on the consequences of publication. For example, publication of reading ages of children in particular schools, or productivity and absenteeism in particular commercial enterprises, could have effects on public reaction and the well-being of participants.

Finally, as a warning against lack of caution in relation to the application of research findings, Sieber and Stanley claim that the combination of new discoveries in genetics and mental testing in the first quarter of the twentieth century contributed to public policy which promoted compulsory sterilization of mentally retarded people, institutionalization, and restrictions on immigration. Several distinguished social scientists contributed, through their research, to such repressive policies.

## Does psychology support the status quo?

Prilleltensky (1989), taking up the issue of social responsibility, argues that psychology, rather than promoting human welfare, might actually hinder social progress by protecting the status quo and the selfish interests of those in power in society. Psychologists, like everyone else, are conditioned intellectually by the belief systems of the culture and unconsciously support an implicit political ideology. Psychologists rarely challenge prevailing beliefs but often actively endorse them.

Such issues are crucially important in a century when psychology appears to be taking over many of the functions formerly supported by religion. But rather than criticise the social order, psychology tends to reinforce and ratify it. Prilleltensky (1989) claims that every organized community has a ruling group which seeks to perpetuate its position through various mechanisms including cultural mechanisms that sustain social order. Psychology has played a part in seeking the causes of action *within the individual* rather than within society at large. This dichotomy between individual and society gives an ideological benefit since the individual is seen as asocial and ahistorical, disconnected from wider sociopolitical contexts. Thus, solutions for human problems are seen within the person rather than in major social change. As examples of psychology's role in sustaining this view, Prilleltensky (1989) cites the testing movement, social Darwinism, individualism, male supremacy, political conformity, and the claim that technology (rather than moral reform) has the capacity to solve human problems. Most psychologists, he claims, are socialized to accept the belief systems of the ruling social class, since they themselves are members of it. Various rites of passage, within (say) the educational system, serve to socialize the individual and help to define self and society.

Again, the belief that psychology is scientifically neutral and value-free helps to represent it as depoliticized, which in turn helps to sustain the dominant ideology. Thus through the guise of objectivity, prescription is seen as description. Prilleltensky (1989) examines the assumptions underlying B. F. Skinner's (e.g., 1974) technology of behaviour and the concept of human engineering; the limitations for social change imposed by functionalism, the emphasis on the organism, and genetics; the naïve neglect of socio-economic factors by humanism, and Carl Rogers's (1951, 1970) apparent belief that the world is full of well-meaning therapists; and cognitivism's focus on perceived rather than external reality. He concludes that psychologists should be more active in entering the debate about what is "the good society"; by making people aware that what we take as facts are actually assumptions, we can educate them to think for themselves.

Research on ethnicity and gender and the failure of ethical codes to be sensitive to the reactions and feelings of minority groups offers an example of ways in which psychological research has served to sustain social roles in society.

## Race and gender as psychological variables

Scarr (1988) argues that "cowardice about minority and gender differences will lead us nowhere" (p. 56). She claims that psychologists studying sensitive issues such as social class or child-rearing practices rarely highlight race or gender as an issue because of the potential consequences for the researcher, such issues being too controversial. Alternatively, having included different ethnic or gender groups in a research design to ensure representativeness of the sample, researchers might post hoc discover differences as an afterthought. Starr claims that both approaches are reprehensible. Psychologists, by ignoring minority groups, might fail to represent those groups fairly, identify their strengths, or create appropriate understandings. Rather than protect such groups, she claims, they damage them. What is needed is good-quality, value-free research, that tells us what society needs to do to help minority groups succeed.

For example, if research questions, influenced by prevailing values, focus on deficiencies or needs, then research outcomes will be negative. If particular gender styles or family arrangements are seen as healthy, then other gender styles or family arrangements (which might well interact with ethnicity) will be shown to be deficient. There is, she claims, relatively little research on the *strengths* of under-represented groups because of the implicit biases in psychologists' belief systems.

Condor (1991) argues that the BPS Principles, focusing on the relationship between experimenter and participant, neglect the possibility that the research might be offensive to particular groups. She cites published studies that use blatantly sexist material, for example, the use of pornographic films in the study of aggression in men. Male participants might not object to such material, but its very use is an insult to women. Denmark et al. (1988) provide a check-list for avoiding sexism in psychological research. Condor argues that such check-lists have actually had little impact, either on research itself, or on the role of journal editors as ethical gatekeepers.

Researchers on ageing have similarly been accused of sustaining stereotypes of elderly incompetence and aiding the stigmatization of elderly people. Schaie (1988) has identified a number of sources of ageist bias in research, and Whitbourne and Hulicka (1990) analyse the content of 139 textbooks, showing that the negative portrayal of elderly people as incompetent in several respects is common, in spite of much research to the contrary.

Thus issues concerning the role of psychologists in society at large, and claims that psychologists are not objective scientists but even pawns of the ruling classes, offer a much greater challenge to psychological ethics than do the more traditional issues of confidentiality, deception, or privacy, for they have major implications for psychology's influence on social policy and social change.

## CONCLUSION

Ethical issues arise in psychology in five major ways: first, in the commitment to the pursuit of truth and the need for integrity in scientific research; second, in the uses (good or ill) to which the results of research might be put; third, in the way psychology projects an image of the person into broader social consciousness; fourth, in selective decisions to conduct research in particular ways and from particular viewpoints, thereby sustaining bias against stigmatized social groups; and finally, in the treatment of participants in the laboratory and other research settings. Learned societies have focused their concerns on the protection of participants, but there is an urgent need to consider the broader issues.

## ACKNOWLEDGEMENTS

I wish to thank the following colleagues, who drew my attention to relevant published material for the preparation of this chapter: Mr Richard Hastings, Dr Stephen MacKeith, Dr Don Marcer, Dr Sheila Payne, and Professor Bob Remington.

## FURTHER READING

American Psychological Association (1982). *Ethical principles in the conduct of research with human participants*. Washington, DC: APA.

British Psychological Society (1991). *Code of conduct, ethical principles and guidelines*. Leicester: BPS.

Bulmer, M. (Ed.) (1982). *Social research ethics*. London: Macmillan.

Fairbairn, S., & Fairbairn, G. (Eds) (1987). *Psychology, ethics and change*. London: Routledge & Kegan Paul.

Prilleltensky, I. (1989). Psychology and the status quo. *American Psychologist, 44,* 795–802.

## REFERENCES

Aitkenhead, M., & Dordoy, J. (1983). Research on the ethics of research. *Bulletin of the British Psychological Society, 36,* 315–318.

Aitkenhead, M., & Dordoy, J. (1985). What the subjects have to say. *British Journal of Social Psychology, 24,* 293–305.

American Psychological Association (1982). *Ethical principles in the conduct of research with human participants*. Washington, DC: APA.

American Psychological Association (1990). Ethical principles of psychologists (amended 2 June 1989). *American Psychologist, 45,* 390–395.

Appelbaum, P. S., & Rosenbaum, A. (1989). *Tarasoff* and the researcher: Does the duty to protect apply in the research setting? *American Psychologist, 44,* 885–894.

Bateson, P. (1986). When to experiment on animals. *New Scientist, 109,* 30–32.

Baumrind, D. (1964). Some thoughts on the ethics of research after reading Milgram's "Behavioral Study of Obedience". *American Psychologist, 19,* 4211–4223.

Baumrind, D. (1971). Principles of ethical conduct in the treatment of subjects: Reaction to the draft report of the committee on ethical standards in psychological research. *American Psychologist, 26,* 887–896.

Brennan, T. (1992). *The interpretation of the flesh: Freud and femininity*. London: Routledge.

British Psychological Society (1990). Ethical principles for conducting research with human participants. *The Psychologist, 3,* 270–272.

British Psychological Society (1991). *Code of conduct, ethical principles and guidelines*. Leicester: BPS.

Ceci, C. J., Peters, D., & Plotkin, J. (1985). Human subjects review, personal values, and the regulation of social science research. *American Psychologist, 40,* 994–1002.

Condor, S. (1991). Sexism in psychological research: A brief note. *Feminism & Psychology, 1,* 430–434.

Denmark, F., Russo, N. F., Frieze, I. H., & Sechzer, J. A. (1988). Guidelines for avoiding sexism in psychological research: A report of the ad hoc committee on nonsexist research. *American Psychologist, 43,* 582–585.

Experimental Psychology Society (1986). *The use of animals for research by psychologists*, London: EPS.

Fletcher, R. (1991). *Science, ideology and the media: The Cyril Burt scandal*. London: Transaction.

Gale, A. (1990). Applying psychology to the psychology degree: Pass with first class honours, or miserable failure? *The Psychologist*, *3*, 483–488.

Gale, A., & Chapman, A. J. (1984). The nature of applied psychology. In A. Gale & A. J. Chapman (Eds) *Psychology and social problems: An introduction to applied psychology* (pp. 1–26). Chichester: Wiley.

Gale, A., & Vetere, A. (1987). Ethical issues in the study of family life. In A. Vetere & A. Gale (Eds) *Ecological studies of family life* (pp. 79–86). Chichester: Wiley.

Gerdes, E. P. (1979). College students' reactions to social psychological experiments involving deception. *Journal of Social Psychology*, *107*, 99–110.

Gray, J. A. (1987). The ethics and politics of animal experimentation. In H. Beloff & A. M. Colman (Eds) *Psychology survey 6* (pp. 218–233). Leicester: British Psychological Society.

Hearnshaw, L. S. (1979). *Cyril Burt: Psychologist*. London: Hodder & Stoughton.

Herzog, H. A. Jr (1988). The moral status of mice. *American Psychologist*, *43*, 473–474.

Joynson, R. B. (1989). *The Burt affair*. London: Routledge.

Kelman, H. C. (1967). Human use of human subjects: The problem of deception in social psychological experiments. *Psychological Bulletin*, *67*, 1–11.

Mead, M. (1928). *Coming of age in Samoa: A psychological study of primitive youth for western civilization*. New York: Morrow.

Mead, M. (1935). *Sex and temperament in three primitive societies*. New York: Morrow.

Mead, M. (1949). *Male and female*. New York: Morrow.

Melton, G. B., & Gray, J. N. (1988). Ethical dilemmas in AIDS research: Individual privacy and public health. *American Psychologist*, *43*, 60–64.

Michaels, T. F., & Oetting, E. R. (1979). The informed consent dilemma: An empirical approach. *Journal of Social Psychology*, *109*, 223–230.

Milgram, S. (1963). Behavioral study of obedience. *Journal of Abnormal and Social Psychology*, *67*, 371–378.

Milgram, S. (1977). Ethical issues in the study of obedience. In S. Milgram (Ed.) *The individual in the social world* (pp. 188–199). Reading, MA: Addison-Wesley.

Miller, N. E. (1985). The value of behavioral research on animals. *American Psychologist*, *40*, 423–440.

Mulvey, E. P., & Phelps, P. (1988). Ethical balances in juvenile justice research and practice. *American Psychologist*, *43*, 669.

Neef, N. A., Iwata, B. A., & Page, T. J. (1986). Ethical standards in behavioral research: A historical analysis and review of publication practices. In A. Poling & R. W. Fuqua (Eds) *Research methods in applied behavior analysis: Issues and advances* (pp. 233–263). New York: Plenum.

Prilleltensky, I. (1989). Psychology and the status quo. *American Psychologist*, *44*, 795–802.

Rogers, C. R. (1951). *Client-centred therapy*. Boston, MA: Houghton Mifflin.

Rogers, C. R. (1970). *Carl Rogers on encounter groups*. New York: Harper & Row.

Rollin, B. E. (1985). The moral status of research animals in psychology. *American Psychologist*, *40*, 920–926.

Scarr, S. (1988). Race and gender as psychological variables: Social and ethical issues. *American Psychologist*, *43*, 56–59.

Schaie, K. W. (1988). Ageism in psychological research. *American Psychologist*, *43*, 179–183.

Schlenker, B. R., & Forsyth, D. R. (1977). On the ethics of psychological research. *Journal of Experimental Social Psychology*, *13*, 369–396.

Schultz, D. P. (1969). The human subject in psychological research. *Psychological Bulletin*, *72*, 214–228.

Sieber, J. E., & Stanley, B. (1988). Ethical and professional dimensions of socially sensitive research. *American Psychologist*, *43*, 49–55.

Silverman, I. (1977). *The human subject in the psychological laboratory*. New York: Pergamon.

Skinner, B. F. (1974). *About behaviorism*. New York: Alfred A. Knopf.

Skinner, L. J., Berry, K. K., Biro, M., & Jackson, T. (1991). Research ethicality: The perceptions of participants and their participation willingness. *Current Psychology: Research & Reviews*, *10*, 79–91.

Wadeley, A. (1991). *Ethics in psychological research and practice*. Leicester: British Psychological Society.

Whitbourne, S. K., & Hulicka, I. M. (1990). Ageism in undergraduate psychology texts. *American Psychologist*, *45*, 1127–1136.

Zimbardo, P. G. (1973). On the ethics on intervention in human psychological research: With special reference to the Stanford prison experiment. *Cognition*, *2*, 243–256.

# GLOSSARY

This glossary is confined to a selection of frequently used terms that merit explanation or comment. Its informal definitions are intended as practical guides to meanings and usages. The entries are arranged alphabetically, word by word, and numerals are positioned as though they were spelled out.

**alternative hypothesis** in statistical tests, a hypothesis that, in contrast to the null hypothesis (q.v.), typically asserts that the independent variable (q.v.) has an effect on the dependent variable (q.v.) that cannot be explained by chance alone. It is also called an experimental or research hypothesis. *See also* significance (statistical).

**analysis of variance** any of a number of statistical techniques for partitioning the variance (q.v.) in experimental data into components to determine whether the differences between samples can be explained by chance.

**arithmetic mean** *see* mean.

**attitude** a fairly stable evaluative response towards a person, object, activity, or abstract concept, comprising a cognitive component (positive or negative perceptions and beliefs), an emotional component (positive or negative feelings), and a behavioural component (positive or negative response tendencies).

**availability heuristic** a heuristic (q.v.) in which the frequency or probability of an event is judged by the number of instances of it that can readily be brought to mind and that are thus cognitively available. It can generate biased or incorrect conclusions, as when people are asked whether the English language contains more words beginning with the letter *r* or more with *r* as the third letter. Most people find it easier to think of instances of the former than the latter and so conclude wrongly that there are more words beginning with *r*.

**case-study** a research method involving a detailed investigation of a single individual or a single organized group, used extensively in clinical psychology and less often in other branches of psychology.

**central limit theorem** in statistics, a theorem showing (roughly) that the sum of any large number of unrelated variables tends to be distributed according to the normal distribution (q.v.). It explains why psychological and biological variables that are due to the additive effects of numerous independently acting causes are distributed approximately normally.

**cohort** from the Latin *cohors*, company of soldiers, a group of people who share some experience or demographic trait in common, especially being of similar age (an age cohort).

**confidence interval** in statistics, a range of values bounded by confidence limits within which there is a specified probability that the true value of a population parameter lies.

113

**confounding** in experimental design (q.v.), the problem that arises when two or more causal variables are not properly controlled so that their independent effects cannot be disentangled.

**construct validity** in psychometrics (q.v.), the validity (q.v.) of a test established by investigating whether it yields the results predicted by the theory underlying the trait that the test purports to measure.

**content validity** in psychometrics (q.v.), the validity (q.v.) of a test estimated via a systematic examination of the items of which it is composed.

**control group** in experimental design (q.v.), a comparison group of subjects who, when the independent variable (q.v.) is manipulated, are not exposed to the treatment that subjects in the experimental group (q.v.) are exposed to, but who in other respects are treated identically to the experimental group, to provide a baseline against which to evaluate the effects of the treatment.

**correlation** in statistics, the relationship between two variables such that high scores on one tend to go with high scores on the other or (in the case of negative correlation) such that high scores on one tend to go with low scores on the other. The usual index of correlation, called the product-moment correlation coefficient and symbolized by $r$, ranges from 1.00 for perfect positive correlation, through zero for uncorrelated variables, to $-1.00$ for perfect negative correlation.

**correlational study** a non-experimental type of research design in which patterns of correlations (q.v.) are analysed.

**criterion validity** in psychometrics (q.v.), the validity (q.v.) of a test determined by applying it to groups of people who are known to differ on the trait that the test purports to measure.

**cross-sectional study** a research design for investigating questions of developmental psychology in which samples of subjects of different ages are studied simultaneously and their behaviour compared. In contrast to a longitudinal study (q.v.), this design does not control for cohort (q.v.) effects.

**culture-fair tests** psychometric tests, especially intelligence tests, that are designed to minimize the biasing influence of cultural knowledge associated with particular ethnic groups, social classes, and other cultural and sub-cultural groups. Culture-free tests (q.v.) are those, if any such exist, entirely free of cultural bias.

**culture-free tests** *see under* culture-fair tests.

**demand characteristics** features of an experimental situation that encourage certain types of behaviour from the subjects and can contaminate the results, especially when this behaviour arises from subjects' expectations or preconceptions or their interpretations of the experimenter's expectations. *Cf.* experimenter effects.

**dependent variable** in experimental design (q.v.), a variable that is potentially liable to be influenced by an independent variable (q.v.). The purpose of an experiment (q.v.) is typically to determine whether one or more independent variables influence one or more dependent variables in a predicted manner.

**descriptive statistics** methods of summarizing numerical data in ways that make them more easily interpretable, including calculations of means (averages), variabilities, and correlations (qq.v.). *Cf.* inferential statistics.

**double-blind study** a research design in which, in order to control for experimenter effects and the effects of demand characteristics (qq.v.), neither the experimenter nor the subjects know, until after the data have been collected, which experimental treatment has been applied to which subjects. This type of design is used, for example, in drug trials, with the help of placebos (q.v.), to avoid contamination of the results from biases and preconceptions on the part of the experimenter or the subjects.

114

**empirical** from the Greek *en*, in, *peira*, trial, derived from observation or experiment rather than speculation or theory.

**equivalent-form reliability** a measure of the reliability (q.v.) of a psychological test based on the correlation (q.v.) between scores obtained on two equivalent versions of the test; if the test measures reliably, and if the equivalent forms really are equivalent, the correlation should be high. *Cf.* split-half reliability, test-retest reliability.

**experiment** a research method whose defining features are manipulation of an independent variable (q.v.) or variables and control of other (extraneous) variables that might influence the dependent variable (q.v.). Experimental methods are uniquely powerful in allowing rigorous examination of causal effects without the uncertainties of other research methods. *See also* control group, experimental group, quasi-experiment.

**experimental design** the general plan of an experiment, including the method of assigning subjects to treatment conditions, controlling extraneous variables, manipulating the independent variable, and of measuring the dependent variable (qq.v.).

**experimental group** in experimental design, a group of subjects exposed to an independent variable (q.v.) in order to examine the causal effect of that variable on a dependent variable (q.v.). *Cf.* control group.

**experimental hypothesis** *see* alternative hypothesis.

**experimenter bias** *see* experimenter effects.

**experimenter effects** biasing effects on the results of an experiment caused by expectations or preconceptions on the part of the experimenter; also called experimenter bias. *Cf.* demand characteristics.

**factor analysis** a statistical technique for analysing the correlations between a large number of variables in order to reduce them to a smaller number of underlying dimensions, called factors, in a manner analogous to the way in which all spectral colours can be reduced to combinations of just three primary colours.

**field experiment** an experiment (q.v.) carried out in a natural setting rather than in the artificial environment of a laboratory.

**field study** a research investigation, not necessarily a field experiment (possibly a non-experimental study) carried out in a natural setting rather in the artificial environment of a laboratory.

**heuristic** from the Greek *heuriskein*, to discover, any of a number of methods of solving complex problems by means of rough-and-ready rules of thumb. *See also* availability heuristic, representativeness heuristic.

**hypothesis** a tentative explanation for a phenomenon, subject to refutation by empirical (q.v.) evidence. *See also*, alternative hypothesis, null hypothesis.

**independent variable** in experimental design (q.v.), a variable that is varied by the experimenter independently of other variables in order to examine its effects on the dependent variable (q.v.).

**inferential statistics** techniques for inferring conclusions about populations on the basis of data from samples. The major objective is usually to decide whether the results of research are statistically significant. *See* significance (statistical).

**interval scale** a scale of measurement in which differences between values can be quantified in absolute terms but the zero point is fixed arbitrarily, a familiar example being temperature. *Cf.* nominal scale, ordinal scale, ratio scale.

**Latin square** in statistics, a square array of numbers or other symbols such that no number or symbol occurs more than once in any row or column.

**longitudinal study** a research design in which the same sample of subjects is examined repeatedly over an extended span of time, typically to investigate problems of developmental psychology. *Cf.* cross-sectional study.

**mean** short for arithmetic mean, the technical word in descriptive statistics (q.v.) for the most common measure of central tendency, popularly known as the average. The mean of a finite set of scores is normally calculated by adding the scores together and then dividing the total by the number of scores. *Cf.* median, mode.

**median** a measure of central tendency in descriptive statistics (q.v.), the middle score in a series of scores arranged in order of magnitude, or the average of the two middle scores if there is an even number of scores. *Cf.* mean, mode.

**meta-analysis** a technique for combining the results of a number of research studies and analysing them statistically as a single data set.

**mode** a measure of central tendency in descriptive statistics (q.v.), the most frequently occurring score among a collection of scores. *Cf.* mean, median.

**multiple regression** a statistical method of analysing the joint and separate influences of several independent variables on a dependent variable (qq.v.).

**naturalistic observation** a research method involving the passive observation of behaviour in naturally occurring situations.

**nominal scale** a discrete method of data classification in which items are not measured or even arranged in order but are merely allocated to different (often numbered) categories as, for example, in assigning numbers to categories of books in a library classification system. *Cf.* interval scale, ordinal scale, ratio scale.

**nonparametric statistics** a branch of statistics that deals with data measured on ordinal or nominal scales (qq.v.) to which ordinary arithmetic operations like addition cannot meaningfully be applied.

**normal distribution** a symmetrical, bell-shaped probability distribution, with the most probable scores concentrated around the mean (average) and progressively less probable scores occurring further from the mean: 68.26 per cent of scores fall within one standard deviation (q.v.) on either side of the mean, 95.44 per cent fall within two standard deviations, and 99.75 fall within three standard deviations. Because of the central limit theorem (q.v.), the normal distribution approximates the observed frequency distributions of many psychological and biological variables and is widely used in inferential statistics (q.v.).

**null hypothesis** in statistical hypothesis testing, the provisional hypothesis that there is no difference or no relationship and that the observed experimental results can be attributed to chance alone. If the statistical test rejects the null hypothesis, then the alternative hypothesis (q.v.) may be entertained and the effect that has been observed may be considered statistically significant. *See also* significance (statistical).

**ordinal scale** a scale of measurement in which data are arranged in order of magnitude but there is no standard measure of degrees of difference between them, for example a ranking of tennis players. *Cf.* interval scale, nominal scale, ratio scale.

**parametric statistics** a branch of statistics concerned with data measured on interval or ratio scales, and therefore suitable for the application of ordinary arithmetic operations such as addition, so that parameters such as the mean and standard deviation (qq.v.) can be meaningfully defined.

116

**placebo** from the Latin word meaning I shall please (the opening words of the Roman Catholic office or service for the dead are *Placebo Domino*, I shall please the Lord), an inactive substance or dummy treatment administered to a control group (q.v.) to compare its effects with those of a real drug or treatment. *See also* double-blind study, placebo effect.

**placebo effect** a positive or therapeutic benefit resulting from the administration of a placebo (q.v.) to someone who believes that the treatment is real.

**population** in statistics, the entire aggregate of individuals from which samples are drawn and to which the results of research investigations may be generalized. *Cf.* sample.

**product-moment correlation coefficient** *see under* correlation.

**psychology** from the Greek *psyche*, mind, *logos*, study, the study of the nature, functions, and phenomena of behaviour and mental experience.

**psychometrics** from the Greek *psyche*, mind, *metron*, measure, mental testing, including IQ, ability, and aptitude testing and the use of psychological tests for measuring interests, attitudes, and personality traits and for diagnosing mental disorders.

**quasi-experiment** any research method that is not strictly experimental but that has some of the features of an experiment (q.v.).

**quota sampling** a non-random method of drawing a sample from a population so that its composition in terms of sex, age, social class, or other demographic characteristics matches the known proportions in the population. *Cf.* random sampling.

**random sampling** any method of drawing a sample from a population in such a way that every member of the population is equally likely to be selected. *Cf.* quota sampling.

**randomization** a technique of experimental design (q.v.) introduced by R. A. Fisher in 1926 in which experimental subjects are assigned to treatment conditions strictly at random in order to control extraneous variables and enable inferential statistics (q.v.) to be used to determine the significance of any differences that are then observed. *See* significance (statistical).

**ratio scale** a scale of measurement in which differences between values can be quantified in absolute terms and a fixed zero point is unambiguously defined, as for example in measurements of length. *Cf.* interval scale, nominal scale, ordinal scale.

**reliability** in psychometrics (q.v.), the consistency and stability with which a measuring instrument performs its function. *See also* equivalent-form reliability, split-half reliability, test-retest reliability. *Cf.* validity.

**representativeness heuristic** a heuristic (q.v.) in which judgements tend to be based on the representative of an instance rather than any other factors affecting its likelihood, for example when people judge a conservatively dressed man with little interest in politics to be an engineer rather than a lawyer even when they know that he was selected from a group composed of 70 per cent lawyers and only 30 per cent engineers.

**research hypothesis** *see* alternative hypothesis.

**response** any behavioural or glandular activity of a person or an animal, especially as a reaction to a stimulus (q.v.).

**sample** a number of individuals selected from a population (q.v.) to test hypotheses about the population or to derive estimates of its characteristics.

**significance (statistical)** a property of the results of an empirical investigation suggesting that they are unlikely to be due to chance factors alone. The 5 per cent level of significance has become conventional in psychology; this means that results are normally considered to be statistically significant if statistical tests show that the probability of obtaining results at least as extreme by chance alone is less than 5 per cent, usually written $p < .05$. *See also* alternative hypothesis, inferential statistics, null hypothesis.

**split-half reliability** a measure of the reliability (q.v.), more specifically the consistency, of a psychological test determined by calculating the correlation (q.v.) between scores obtained on half the test items, arbitrarily chosen, with scores obtained on the other half; if the test measures consistently, the correlation should be high. *Cf.* equivalent-form reliability, test-retest reliability.

**standard deviation** in descriptive statistics (q.v.), a measure of dispersion or variability expressed in the same units as the scores themselves, equal to the square root of the variance (q.v.).

**standard score** the score on any measuring instrument expressed in units of standard deviations (q.v.) of the distribution of scores in the population, also called a z-score.

**statistical significance** *see* significance (statistical).

**stimulus** (pl. stimuli) any objectively discernable event capable of evoking a response (q.v.) in an organism.

**subjects** from the Latin *sub*, under, *jacere*, to throw, people or other organisms whose behaviour or mental experience is investigated in psychological research.

**survey methods** research methods for investigating the distribution of attitudes, opinions, and other psychological attributes in specific sections of a population or in whole populations.

**t-test** in inferential statistics (q.v.), a test to establish the significance of a difference between the means of two samples.

**test-retest reliability** a measure of the reliability (q.v.) of a psychological test, more specifically its stability, determined by calculating the correlation (q.v.) between scores obtained by a group of subjects on the test on two separate occasions; if the test measures stably, and if the psychological characteristic being measured is stable over time, the correlation should be high. *Cf.* equivalent-form reliability, split-half reliability.

**validity** from the Latin *validus*, strong, in psychometrics (q.v.), the degree to which a measuring instrument measures what it purports to measure. *See also* construct validity, content validity, criterion validity. *Cf.* reliability.

**variability** in statistics, the degree to which a set of scores is scattered. Thus two sets of scores with identical means (averages) may have widely different variabilities. The usual measures of variability are the variance and the standard deviation (qq.v.).

**variable** anything that is subject to variation; in psychological research, any stimulus, response, or extraneous factor that is not necessarily fixed and may influence the results of the research. *See also* dependent variable, independent variable.

**variance** in descriptive statistics (q.v.), a measure of the dispersion or variability (q.v.) of a set of scores; it is equal to the mean (average) of the squared deviations of the scores from their mean. *See also* standard deviation.

**z-score** another name for a standard score (q.v.).

# INDEX